Net Gain in Construction: Using the Internet in the Construction Industry

Edward Finch, MSc PhD
University of Reading, UK

BUTTERWORTH HEINEMANN

OXFORD AUCKLAND BOSTON JOHANNESBURG MELBOURNE NEW DELHI

Butterworth-Heinemann
Linacre House, Jordan Hill, Oxford OX2 8DP
225 Wildwood Avenue, Woburn, MA 01801-2041
A division of Reed Educational and Professional Publishing Ltd

$\mathcal{R}$ A member of the Reed Elsevier plc group

First published 2000

© Edward Finch 2000

British Library Cataloguing in Publication Data
A catalogue record for this book is available from the British Library

Library of Congress Cataloguing in Publication Data
A catalogue record for this book is available from the British Library

ISBN 0 7506 5052 4

Typeset by Academic & Technical Typesetting, Bristol
Printed and bound in Great Britain by Biddles Ltd
www.biddles.co.uk

FOR EVERY TITLE THAT WE PUBLISH, BUTTERWORTH-HEINEMANN
WILL PAY FOR BTCV TO PLANT AND CARE FOR A TREE.

Contents

Preface   vii
Acknowledgements   ix
List of figures   x

Chapter 1 – Creating a learning organization in construction   **1**
  Questions addressed in this chapter   1
  Knowledge and communication   1
  Learning organizations in construction   2
  Information in construction   2
  Construction under pressure   4
  The Internet-enabled learning organization   7
  Primacy of the whole   8
  The community nature of individuals   9
  Creative power of language   10
  Four functions of the mind   11
  A roadmap   12
  Key points from this chapter   14

Chapter 2 – Creating a virtual value chain   **15**
  Questions addressed in this chapter   15
  Marketplace and marketspace   15
  Virtual value chain   16
  Three stages of virtual value adding   18
  New economics of information   19
  From physical to information resources   19
  Transformation of the economics of information   20
  Zero-sum game   23
  Internet strategy and fit   24
  Key points from this chapter   27

Chapter 3 – Creating visibility   **28**
  Questions addressed in this chapter   28
  Visibility and the learning organization   29
  Static and dynamic information   29
  Bechtel Corporation   31
  Document-driven knowledge systems   34
  Who needs machine interpretation?   35
  Birth of markup languages   36
  Web-based markup   37
  Arrival of XML   37
  Overcoming information overload   39
  Key points from this chapter   40

Chapter 4 – Creating new services   **41**
  Questions addressed in this chapter   41
  Mirroring capabilities   41
  Internet-enabled design   42
  Internet-enabled CAD   43
  CAD browsers   46
  Existing CAD browsers   46
  Internet aware CAD data   47
  Shortcomings of CAD   48
  Object modelling   49
  Creating the industrial virtual enterprise   53
  Interoperability   57
  Replacing face-to-face interaction in design and construction 57
  Understanding face-to-face communication   58
  Nonverbal communication   60
  Technical trade-offs   61
  Internet-based real-time video   62
  Video-as-data   63
  Video for connection   63
  Reality of mirroring the face-to-face experience   64
  Taywood Engineering   64
  Key points from this chapter   67

Chapter 5 – Creating customer communities   **68**
  Questions addressed in this chapter   68
  Introduction   68
  Hans Haenlein Architects   69

Power of the on-line community   73
Examples of on-line discussions   74
The future of on-line communities   78
Key points from this chapter   82

Chapter 6 – Creating trust   **83**
Questions addressed in this chapter   83
Introduction   83
Transaction costs and opportunism   84
Trust and virtuality   84
Security and the Internet   85
Dimensions of electronic security   87
Encryption concepts   88
Firewalls   90
Firewall policies   93
Virtual private networks   94
Partnering and trust   94
Benefits of trust   97
Key points from this chapter   97

Chapter 7 – Creating trade   **99**
Questions addressed in this chapter   99
Dodo strategy   99
Broad view of e-commerce   100
Stages of the buying process   101
Electronic data interchange in construction   102
Plug-and-play organizations using XML   104
Software agents   106
Identifying e-commerce applications   111
Extranets   113
Two types of extranet   113
Summary   115
Key points from this chapter   116

Chapter 8 – Creating an Internet architecture   **117**
Questions addressed in this chapter   117
What is the problem?   117
What are the options?   118
What is aecXML?   120
Types of information encompassed in aecXML   122

AecXML schema and emerging XML capabilities 123
Elements in the aecXML specification 126
Demise of the document 128
From paperless to documentless 129
Designing an XML-based information management system 131
Content repository 134
Key points from this chapter 137

Chapter 9 – Creating an Internet system specification **138**
Questions addressed in this chapter 138
Importance of planning 138
Stages involved 140
Stage 1: Organizing 141
Stage 2: Baseline views 143
Stage 3: Target definition 146
Key points from this chapter 148

Chapter 10 – Creating the future **149**
Questions addressed in this chapter 149
Introduction 149
Document driven or people driven? 150
What next? 153
How ready is your business? 154
Deep learning 155
People make businesses 156

Directory of expertise – Internet in construction 157

Glossary 162

References 176

Index 179

Preface

The construction industry is unique in its inertia to change. The transient nature of construction projects and the teams that engage in them create an environment of continual upheaval – one that discounts any long-term economies and learning cycles. Unlike manufacturers, who can fine-tune processes and create permanent production systems, construction firms are relegated to a nomadic existence in a wilderness of changing project infrastructures. But one technology is likely to transform this – a technology based on open standards. It will enable the creation of industry conglomerations very different from the ones we see today. The economics of information, dominated by considerations of span and control are being redefined. Information, previously tied to the physical value chain, is being liberated to create completely new *virtual value chains*. The laws governing the behaviour of virtual value chains are dramatically different from the *physical value chains* the construction industry is accustomed to. New opportunities will be created in what will be a 'deconstruction of the construction value chain'.

These transformational developments concern not just information technology departments. Senior executives are having to take stock of firms' strategic position in the construction value chain. It is with this in mind that this book was conceived. The principles of Internet technology are often seen as complex and alienating for decision-makers in the construction industry. The abundance of jargon, hype and overnight obsolescence deters managers from taking positive action regarding the Internet. Moreover, concerns about even more information being available fill managers with a sense of dread rather than excitement. Managers are tempted to ignore it or delegate it to the 'techie' department. This book is aimed at all managers in the construction industry who have some involvement in their firm's long-term strategy. It takes as a basic tenet that their management skills are far more consequential than any technical know-how. From this tenet, the book translates the new capability of the Internet into a meaningful strategic framework.

The construction industry will no longer be considered an also-ran against the sophistication of the manufacturing industries. It will become one of the most responsive and innovative users of the new net technologies. With it will arise a demand for some of the best thinkers and managers in any industry.

One event which prompted me to write this book was an occasion when I was invited as a 'fly-on-the-wall' visitor to what was an internal meeting of a large contractor. During the meeting it became evident that the total sum of their internet strategy was to outsource. This struck a chord of some concern for me – a realization that IT managers are making decisions that will have implications reaching far beyond the IT department. One point that is evident is that although many other industries have begun to embrace the Internet as a 'social' phenomenon, the design and construction industries still acknowledge it as a 'technological' phenomenon. As a social phenomenon its potential as an agent for change is considerably greater.

This book presents a theory of Internet development in construction. Here the emphasis is on the original Greek root word of theory, *theo-rós*, meaning 'spectator'. This is derived in turn from the same root word as 'theatre'. Thus, as Senge (1990) puts it,

> human beings invent theories for the same basic reason they invent theatre – to bring out into a public space a play of ideas that might help us better understand our world.

It is in this frame of mind that I have written this book – as a play of possibilities and ideas which new advances in communication offer the modern construction industry.

Edward Finch

Acknowledgements

The author would like to pay tribute to family and colleagues who have supported me during this endeavour.

Thanks should also be extended to the various construction organizations that have helped in the preparation of case studies and in providing invaluable advice.

I would particularly like to acknowledge the city of Belo Horizonté, Brazil, where I have resided as a very happy guest during my time writing this book.

List of figures

Fig. 1.1 Barriers to information transfer in construction.

Fig. 1.2 The deep learning cycle.

Fig. 1.3 A holistic view of reasoning in construction processes.

Fig. 1.4 'Roadmap' of the book.

Fig. 2.1 EPSRC IMI Generic Design and Construction Process Protocol.

Fig. 2.2 Stages of development of the virtual value chain and its relationship with the deep learning cycle.

Fig. 2.3 Trade-off between 'richness' and 'reach' in a traditional model of information economics.

Fig. 2.4 Traditional hierarchical project structure.

Fig. 2.5 Hyperarchy – deconstructed value chain of construction project.

Fig. 2.6 Productivity frontier and the state of best practice.

Fig. 2.7 Activity–systems map for a design-build firm specializing in factory units.

Fig. 3.1 Moving from presentation to semantics.

Fig. 3.2 Unpacking an XML document.

Fig. 4.1 Illustration of CAD intrastructure involving different providers and users (based on Regli, 1997).

Fig. 4.2 Three levels of design infrastructure and the new engineering services (based on Regli, 1997).

Fig. 4.3 NIIIP demonstration project system design.

Fig. 4.4 Supported operations in the NIIIP project.

Fig. 4.5 Content and process elements of face-to-face conversation.

Fig. 4.6 Real-time video applications.

Fig. 5.1 Visualization of discussion groups using CommunityOrganizer.

Fig. 5.2 Defining user profiles using CommunityOrganizer.

Fig. 6.1 Symmetric key system (based on Bhimani, 1996).

Fig. 6.2 Asymmetric public key encryption systems.

Fig. 6.3 Metaphor of firewall as a medieval castle.

Fig. 6.4 Categories of firewall system.
Fig. 6.5 The evolution of trust (based on Shapiro *et al.*, 1992).
Fig. 7.1 Use of the eCo Server concept to generate XML-based exchange documents (based on Glushko *et al.*, 1999).
Fig. 7.2 Framework of e-commerce exploitation in construction.
Fig. 8.1 System architecture for XML document management.
Fig. 8.2 Using the XML editor Framemaker + SGML to create content.
Fig. 8.3 XMetal editor making use of the XML database bridge with Astoria.
Fig. 8.4 Context management – the tree structure based in Astoria.
Fig. 8.5 History of an XML document in Astoria showing a change in content for the Title component.

1

Creating a learning organization in construction

Questions addressed in this chapter

- What forms of communication do we rely on in the construction industry?

- Can these forms of communication be translated to a virtual environment?

- What are the benefits and possible dangers of moving towards virtual communication?

- How can we ensure that our organization does not simply allow corporate knowledge to diffuse out to competitors in our attempts to achieve intra-organizational co-operation in construction projects?

- How do we increase the longevity of acquired construction know-how, so that it continues to be reused and we learn from our mistakes?

- How will virtual communication across the Internet affect people working in the construction industry?

Knowledge and communication

What direction is your firm taking on the path of knowledge management? Without some answers to this question it is difficult to embark on an Internet strategy. But how do we distinguish between data and information, knowledge and insight? This chapter begins by looking at how the construction industry relies on information of many kinds – from hard data to tacit loosely defined knowledge, how information is fundamentally distinct from data, and how it embraces many subtle interactions in the real world which are often so difficult to reproduce in the digital world. We will see how *lean*, uncodified information is predominant in many types of exchange in construction. This creates a ceaseless back-and-forth exchange. More importantly, it deprives firms of the ability to create a corporate intelligence that moves beyond the next contract and the next project. This chapter explores the idea of the 'learning organization'. It offers a framework to enable firms to create a sustainable position in a construction industry increasingly dominated by information rather than physical resources. We see how the 'deep learning model' is enabled by Internet technology, provided a suitable Internet strategy is thought through. Later chapters show how Internet-based communication can be developed to meet the very exacting requirement for rich information exchange in construction.

Learning organizations in construction

The Internet has prompted a radically new way of doing business in construction. Firms are not just looking to reproduce old practices as digital mirrors. Managers are realizing that the technology enables a fundamentally new way of working. It challenges the way that firms interact on the value chain. It prompts a re-evaluation of trading relationships. It stimulates an exploration of wholly new opportunities for products and services. Information is no longer a supporting element of the value-adding process in construction – it is a way of creating new value for the customer (client). Firms are having to revisit every part of their business as the virtual value-chain supplants the physical value chain.

We will see that only by becoming *learning organizations* can we truly harness the possibilities offered by the Internet and play a vital part in the construction process.

Information in construction

Examine any conversation between two people and you soon realize that there is much more going on than first appears. Conversation is significantly more complex than the electronic exchange of bits and bytes between computers. Think about a buyer engaged in a purchasing discussion with a materials supplier – searching for a fair price. The silences often tell more than the periods of talking. What is not said is often more important than what is said. All the assumptions and previous experiences that the two parties have, create a greatly distilled exchange that relies on past experience and shared professional expertise. The information itself does not tell the whole story. Besides hard information, other issues such as trust and common values are revealed – will the supplier provide the goods on time? As we move towards the virtual exchange of information how do we capture the subtleties of such information?

Many construction firms have not truly committed themselves to the concept of the Internet. Why is this? Invariably it results from a flawed belief that successful Internet implementation is a technical endeavour. Nothing could be further from the truth. As early as 1949 Weaver (reproduced as a special 50th edition in Shannon and Weaver, 1999) pointed out the three critical factors that determine the successful transfer of information.

- *Technical factors* – The more we can codify or structure information the more rapidly and extensively it can be communicated. An example of this might be a building code or building contract which attempts to distil information into a structured consistent format. The result is an unambiguous, concise and standard document.
- *Semantic factors* – The more codified the information transmitted, the smaller the number of people (specialists) who can understand it or interpret its meaning. Without the knowledge base to decipher the information, the contents of a message are useless. We see this all the time in complex industries such as construction. Construction lawyers have a short-hand way of communicating, which to others sounds like jargon. A building contract document is an example of a highly codified piece of information. Similarly, a numerical analysis of structural load provides a highly codified statement from a structural engineer but can only be understood by others of a similar discipline.
- *Effectiveness factor* – How can you send information to someone choosing not to listen? Can you still call it information if that is the case? Who can receive information from someone intent on misleading the recipient? Many books on information technology are based on the naive assumption that information is inherently good and shared freely. Yet in construction there is a surfeit of misleading information or of information people choose not to share, despite the fact that the information might help others to bring a building product into realization.

By pushing with one of these factors we can reduce the effectiveness of the other two so there are inevitably trade-offs between them.

The Internet allows messages to whiz around the world almost instantaneously. It is a diffuse technology allowing an unlimited number of people to receive information. Well, perhaps things are not as simple as this. A distinction must be made between data and information. *Data* only becomes *information* when the recipient comes to share a common understanding with the sender as a result of a message. In construction there are a multiplicity of barriers to successful information transfer

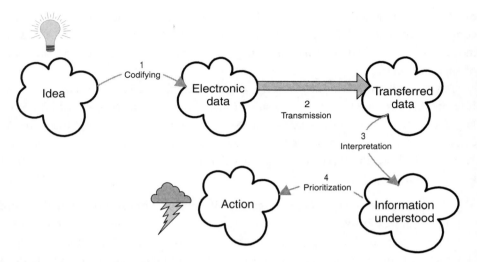

Fig. 1.1 Barriers to information transfer in construction.

and this applies to electronic and traditional information transfer. Speedy transfer of electronic data does not overcome all these barriers. Revisiting the three aspects of information – technical, semantic and effectiveness factor – we see that fast communication only deals with the first aspect of information diffusion, i.e. technical. If we fail to make information intelligible to a wider audience its value is lost. In the absence of a motive to use or respond to the information it does not matter how quickly it travels. This is the essence of understanding Internet strategy planning for construction and the reason why this book devotes so much space to the *semantic* and *effectiveness* factors.

Figure 1.1 shows the information transfer cycle from (1) codifying, (2) transmission, (3) interpretation, to (4) prioritization. Using this model one can quickly see that anyone intent on transferring information successfully cannot concentrate on stage (2). This is the stage that is often seen as being the only contribution of the Internet. We will see that *transmission* is the most trivial and least problematic aspect of the transfer process. The Internet needs to be exploited at every stage of the process.

Construction under pressure

The conventional model of the construction process is under severe stress. This tension is evident in the many forms of contract which attempt to regulate the construction process but which are tied to a form of construction which was prevalent at the early part of the twentieth century. Inevitably, the world has moved on.

Many information systems being used in design and construction slavishly adhere to an outdated transaction process and the strain is beginning to show.

Many of the pressures are driven by client pressures, from organizations having to operate in an increasingly turbulent commercial world. Many stakeholders are adding their voice to the chorus. Buildability, maintainability, recyclability, usability – even crashability! Contractors, facilities managers, building users, and environmentalists are just some of the people who want to have the listening ear of the designer. To satisfy these diverse needs, buildings are invariably becoming more complex. Added to this are the increasing pressures of organizations operating in a dynamic and uncertain environment. Clients such as retailers need fast construction cycles to make sure that they are first to market. Whether it is a retailer wishing to complete a shop fit-out for the Christmas season or microprocessor manufacturer mobilizing for the next generation of silicon chips, time is often the factor that determines success or failure. The building or refurbishment programme is the only thing that stands in the way.

Pietroforte (1997) highlighted just how complex the construction process has become. In his study of façade systems he observed how much of the design responsibility gets passed on to contractors, subcontractors and manufacturers – people who traditionally have not been involved in the design process. The production of thin stone-veneered cladding involves many independent parties who need to coordinate their efforts. Fabrication, assembly and erection result from the cooperative involvement of several design groups. The lead time involved in this effort is considerable, rarely being less than 3 years. The initial contract document may be based on performance specifications, scope designs or incomplete design documents. Given the complexity of the process Pietroforte (1997) argues that

> the shop drawings . . . may lead to a final product that is aesthetically consistent with, but functionally different from what was described in the working drawings and specifications. The difference leaves a significant interpretive leeway as to whether the proposed engineering solutions match the performance or design intents described in the contract documents.

The architectural representation of the façade system is of one single entity. In the generation of shop drawings, the real situation was that four separate sets had to be developed, all by different subcontractors and manufacturers. All this requires complex transactions involving iterative exchanges with many review documents. Moreover, the separate representation of the various components, including granite veneer panels, supporting steel trusses, windows, insulation and drainage made the task of functional continuity very exacting. This is just one example of how complex the construction process is. Many of the problems arise from a dependence on *lean*, uncodified information necessitating a ceaseless back-and-forth interaction.

Information transfer may involve a simple one-to-one transaction or may involve many recipients, giving rise to diffuse information that permeates throughout a company or across many companies involved in a project. We will see later in the book how significant the Internet is in terms of diffusion of information. It raises the possibility of fundamentally different forms of construction organizations and methods for procuring buildings.

Many information media are used in construction. Some types, such as drawings, whether stored electronically or on paper, are rather poor at telling us what we need to know, whether we are air-conditioning engineers, cost engineers or whatever specialism we have. Even with modern CAD technology, we are still reduced to using a combination of lines, dots and surfaces. The metaphor of the 'drawing board' still persists in an electronic form. We still have not cast off the shackles of paper-based technology. In this sense, we can say that the information lacks richness – the information is *lean*. For many applications this may suffice, where information is certain and the requirements of the recipients are clearly defined. However, more often than not, the poverty of information in drawings necessitates a whole gamut of additional interactions including requests for clarification and face-to-face meetings. The recipient often has difficulty in uncodifying the information – they might be from a different profession or have a different view of the requirements. Furthermore, the design itself says nothing about the intent of the designer. Why was a piece of ducting placed there and not here? Perhaps there was a good reason – to avoid clashing with other services. Or perhaps it was put there for no good reason at all – the designer may not have been aware that, for the recipient, its proposed position is less efficient. Lean or low-codified communication media strains under the requirements of modern construction – the need for personalized and synchronous communication. Only by introducing more interactive communication methods can we overcome these deficiencies, using *rich* interaction including the old and established method of 'talking to one another'.

However, rich interaction is achieved at a price. It involves a considerable infrastructure which, until the advent of the Internet, has impeded the diffusion process. Large construction organizations have put great faith in the creation of mammoth codification processes which distil know-how. But, as Pietroforte (1997) points out, 'the use of high-codified information would decrease communication costs and accelerate information diffusion, but at the same time it would entail significant development and learning investments, whose returns must be verified'.

The argument here is that learning organizations in construction hold the key to success. This book is all about the creation of learning organizations in construction – and the role played by the Internet in achieving this goal.

The Internet-enabled learning organization

An Internet strategy that is not aligned with an organizational strategy is bound to become a beached whale. For this reason, this book takes as its starting point the concept of the 'learning organization'. As we shall see, applying the principles of learning organizations greatly increases the potency of Internet technology in design or construction firms. It makes it not just a helpful technology but a key resource.

Give me a lever long enough and I can move the world. (Archimedes)

The 'learning organization' is a phrase coined by Mintzberg (1979) and popularized by Senge (1990). Its basic tenet states that there is no sustainable competitive advantage today other than organizational learning. In other words, a company can only compete if it can learn faster than its competitors. In order to be successful organizations must overcome their learning disabilities and develop as learning organizations. Numerous definitions have been used including:

Organisational learning occurs through shared insights, knowledge and mental models...and builds on past knowledge and experience – that is, on memory (Strata, 1989)

Organisations are seen as learning by encoding inferences from history into routines that guide behaviour (Levitt and March, 1988)

Organisational learning means the process of improving actions through better knowledge and understanding (Fiol and Lyles, 1985)

The idea of the learning organization is at odds with the make-up of many construction firms. This includes the way that they interact in the market place, the constraints imposed upon them by contractual methods and the way they use their most important assets – people. As we are thrown into a shifting environment our ability to respond is often far short of what is required. Diminishing profit margins, loss of personnel, dilution of expertise are all symptomatic. The concept of the learning organization provides a tool for construction and design firms to embrace change. It is not a quick-fix solution but one that requires a close examination of established and outmoded ways of doing things.

Perhaps you can recall a great design or construction team you have worked with. At the outset this team is nothing more than a group of individuals. However, through the passage of time the team begins to develop the knowledge of working as a whole. Team members acquire new skills and abilities, and this in turn alters their level of awareness and sensibilities. As time progresses, this ability to see and experience the world differently leads to a new set of beliefs and assumptions. In

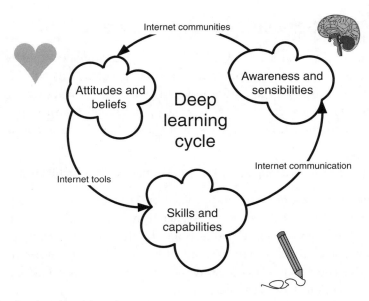

Fig. 1.2 The deep learning cycle.

learning organizations, this progression forms part of a continuing learning cycle that begins again with further development of skills and capabilities. Figure 1.2 illustrates how the Internet can be superimposed on this learning cycle. All too often, the Internet is confined to the informing aspect, involving the shuttling of hard data. However, we can see that by using this model we acquire a much more human centred view that taps into the very heart of a construction firm's activities.

What are the underlying principles of learning organizations? The works of Kofman and Senge (1993) and Senge (1990) state the importance of a common frame of reference. This view of the organization involves three key concepts: (1) the primacy of the whole, (2) the community nature of the self, and (3) the generative power of language.

Primacy of the whole

This concept implies that relationships are more fundamental than things and that wholes are of a fundamentally greater significance than the constituent parts.

Consider a building – we might think of it as a machine with decomposable elements. Is it made up of substructure, superstructure, internal finishes, fittings and services? Of walls, roofs and interior settings? Of structural and non-structural elements? Of passive, active and hybrid systems? Of public and private space? Obviously, the categories we choose are dependent on our own professional backgrounds as architects, cost engineers, maintenance managers or building users.

What makes a building a building is not defined by the constituent parts. A cruise liner also has a substructure, superstructure, internal finishes and services. Thus the function of the building only exists in the function and design of the whole.

As buildings become more complex they come to resemble more and more the characteristics of living systems rather than machines. As Senge (1990) points out, it is nonsense to suggest that we can understand what it is to be human by dissecting the human body. We may well find that it is composed of skin, bones, muscle, organs and nervous tissue, but does this capture what it means to be human? The same dilemma faces building designers. We are often constrained by the need to partition work into individual work packages. As a result, we create 'unwholesome' buildings. The advent of facilities management as a professional fraternity was in many ways a direct challenge to this process. Buildings were clearly not performing, primarily because they were being designed as mechanical systems in a situation that clearly required an organic living system as a solution. The relationships between services and structure are now primordial to the things themselves – the air conditioning units or the beam design. Antagonism has also been evident in the design of services. We have traditionally thought of air-conditioning systems as a way of 'fixing problems'. The deficiencies in the original structural design in terms of thermal mass, level of glazing and orientation are cancelled out by heavy investment in oversized air-conditioning plant. However, by exploring the interrelatedness we come to understand how the external environment interacts with a building's internal climate. How we can offset rapid changes in the outside temperature regime by using greater thermal mass? How we can reduce thermal load by the use of natural shading devices such as trees? So we see that by restating the primacy of the whole we are forced to consider interrelatedness. We no longer tolerate the idea of quick technological fixes such as oversized air-conditioning plant.

Appreciating that interrelatedness is so important we immediately understand the significance of the Internet. This is the very thing that it enables. A capacity to enmesh relationships – whether we are talking about organizational relationships or relationships that exist in our design solution.

The community nature of individuals

The construction industry throughout the world is tied to professional identities. We are architects or civil engineers or builders. This preoccupation with professional identity emerges from our tendency to see the individual as primordial to the 'community' or project team. In construction, this process is perhaps more complex. The demarcation is between our own organization and others involved with a particular project. Any project participant can be seen as having 'a point of view that unifies the flow of experience into a coherent narrative'. Each one of the organizations involved in the project has its own narrative. However, the consequence of this ascendancy of the ego in the construction process is that we see the community as nothing but a network of contractual commitments that control economic exchanges. If, however, we recognize the importance of 'community' in the construction process, we immediately open up possibilities for beneficial changes. Partnering is one such example. This is attracting considerable interest in the construction industry because it allows organizations to change how they do business. In this context we no longer see people from other organizations as objects for our use. Instead we view them as fellow human beings capable of influencing and responding to our own values – individuals with whom we can learn and change.

For an Internet strategy, our understanding of loyalty, trust and commitment to learn with other organizations is inevitably expressed by our approach to information exchange and disclosure. Openness means not just being willing to share our own information, but more deeply – being open to the ideas of others.

Creative power of language

The construction process is often thought of as a very physical process. However, anyone who has been involved in projects will know how they are replete with uncertainties. The truth is we can never know what is really real. With the best cost forecasting model and the most precise programme, we are bound to a level of uncertainty. On a more fundamental level, everything we do in turn impacts on a project so we are never passive observers. This touches on the uncertainty principle derived by the physicist Heisenberg in 1927 who found from observations at an atomic level that 'we can never measure the world without changing it'. Thus in a general sense we can say that our language (communication) interacts with our direct experiences and the reality we bring forth arises from that interaction.

When we sit at a programming meeting or a work progress meeting we are confronted with multiple interpretations of the real world. We often seek to determine what is right, when in fact there is no right; the challenge is to seek the interpretations that are most suitable for a particular purpose, accepting that the idea of a correct interpretation is meaningless.

All too often we try to develop a level of certainty in construction projects which robs us of the capacity to wonder, to innovate – that stifles our ability to see different interpretations and new possibilities for doing things. The antagonistic nature of the construction process can be traced to these root belief systems that become rigid, intractable and self-protective.

How do we develop an Internet system that supports multiple interpretations of the real world – one that is not blinkered by the idea of right answers? We will see how various encoding systems such as SGML (standard generalized markup language) can be used to support this kind of multiple interpretation. Such solutions liberate us from procedural technologies (such as expert systems) which try to embody the right answer.

Four functions of the mind

If we are using information to support the functions of the mind, in what ways do we exercise our minds in design or construction activities? If we are to believe many of the technocrats' views of the future, we will soon be able to displace most office-based activities with virtual working. Information in this sense is purely a resource to enable thinking – other activities of the mind are somehow irrelevant. If we are able to transfer all the design drawings a contractor should be able to get on with the job. If a building services engineer produces a complete air-conditioning specification a cost engineer should be able to price it. This reduces the role of the Internet to one of simple hard-data transfer. But this view is strikingly different from reality. To achieve virtual working we are asking much more than the ability to transfer documents and programmes. To obtain a holistic view of interactions in the design and construction processes we should consider the four functions of the mind described by Jung and Hull (1969). This model applies not only to individual intelligence, but also to corporate and community intelligence.

The four functions of the mind are (Figure 1.3):

- *Thinking* – This allows us to come to conclusions about the real world, based on reasoning and real-life observation. Invariably, it is for this function that we look to information technology to provide the raw material.

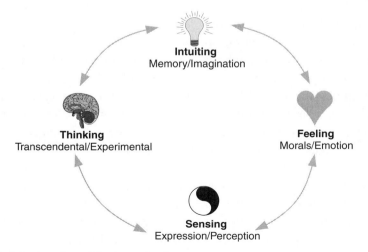

Intuiting
Memory/Imagination

Thinking
Transcendental/Experimental

Feeling
Morals/Emotion

Sensing
Expression/Perception

Fig. 1.3 A holistic view of reasoning in construction processes.

- *Sensing* – We can think of 'sensing information' as information that has not been subject to interpretation (compared with 'thinking' data). We, the user, are left to make sense of what the information is telling us. The increasing use of multimedia and real-time information allows us to experience sensation remotely almost as if we were there ourselves.
- *Intuiting* – Memory and imagination form part of our own make-up as professionals. We have unique experiences, often unrecorded, often difficult to articulate. But we make use of them repeatedly in decision-making. Indeed, evidence suggests the more important the decision the more we come to rely on intuitive reasoning over and above conventional thinking. Does our Internet strategy embrace or exclude this activity?
- *Feeling* – As with any industry, people involved in the construction industry are influenced by morals, and emotion. Any virtual solution that fails to recognize the role of feeling is unlikely to flourish in a full sense.

In later chapters we will see Internet capabilities that harness not only the thinking processes that have often received too much attention at the expense of others. We will consider the strategies for interacting effectively in a virtual context, supporting all aspects of the individual and corporate mind.

A roadmap

The following chapters look in turn at how we can create learning organizations that support every aspect of design and construction firms. Whether we are looking at the individual, corporate or increasingly the enterprise level – the Internet can indeed support the range of human activities so important to the success of the construction industry (Figure 1.4).

Chapter 2 begins by considering a powerful change in information economics that will stimulate the creation of the *virtual value chain*. How do we go about creating the virtual value chain? In Chapter 3 we focus on the 'thinking' aspect of the mind and how codification of Internet information will enable firms to create visibility, both within and outside their own firms. Chapter 4 moves towards the 'sensing' of information and how firms can create new services that allow the exchange of information that is not document-driven. Chapter 5 considers the concept of 'community' on the Internet and how firms are having to revisit their entire business model in response to this – communities that will support every element of human and corporate development, including the 'emotional' part. In Chapter 6 we look at trust, a popular issue in the construction industry today, but something that also affects our approach to Internet security, copyright and the ownership of information. We will see how the intuiting aspect of past experiences and loyalty play a

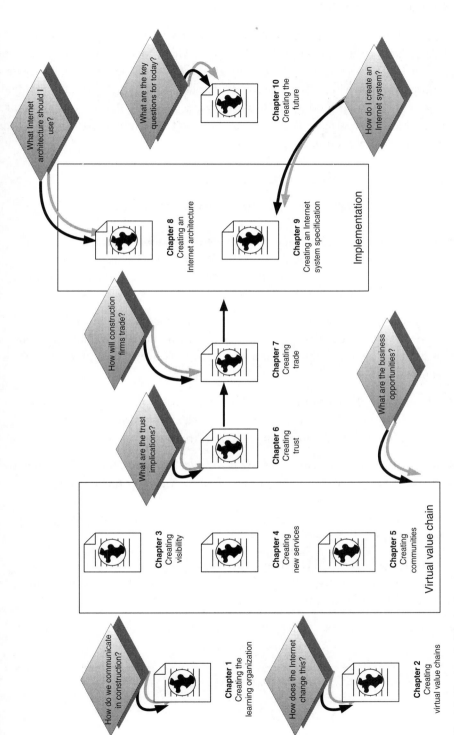

Fig. 1.4 'Roadmap' of the book.

part in the creation of trust – not only in the physical world but the virtual world as well. This chapter links closely with Chapter 7, which focuses on more pragmatic issues of creating trade. How can we bring all these capabilities together to create a plug-and-play construction firm. The final chapter looks at how we as individuals can bring about changes today that will affect our company's success in the future. What economic and structural changes underlie Internet innovation and how can we take steps in preparation for these changes?

KEY POINTS FROM THIS CHAPTER

- The construction industry needs to move from simply reproducing paper-based processes in an electronic form. This means fully realizing the features of electronic material that enable machine–machine and person–machine communication.

- Translating established construction business processes to an electronic virtual counterpart is not without its hazards, because not all information is hard information. Information may need to convey feeling, intuition or sensory data.

- The Internet threatens to overwhelm the construction industry with too much information. The challenge is to encode information that can be efficiently filtered, removing obsolete and irrelevant data.

- Knowledge management is the key to survival. Firms capable of creating a corporate knowledge system that has a lifespan greater than that of individual staff are likely to have a sustainable advantage. Co-operative working with project partners needs careful consideration regarding the diffusion of such expertise.

- Part of knowledge management entails a lifecycle approach to information. Lessons learnt from earlier projects should be captured and made visible to subsequent projects.

- A successful Internet strategy is one that addresses the needs of employees, involving them in a creative learning cycle.

2

Creating a virtual value chain

Questions addressed in this chapter

- Does the Internet offer anything more than a publishing medium for the construction industry?

- What do we mean by the value chain and how does it differ from the supply chain?

- What impact will the Internet have on the construction value chain?

- What significance do new open standards have in terms of the *economics of information*?

- What are the implications for the size of construction firms?

- What will the prevailing economic rules of engagement be if the Internet is to be used more extensively in the construction industry?

- What strategic position should construction firms be taking in order to fit the new order?

Marketplace and marketspace

In 1573 Philip II set about codifying the Spanish Crown's concept of how cities in the New World should be built. Large urban centres already existed in Mexico and Peru where indigenous populations had existed for centuries. But within a century planned colonial cities that were European in culture and architecture had become established. By the use of ordinances and detailed land surveys, large cities like Mexico City were designed from scratch. Not only this – they were designed remotely – by planners in

Spain who had never set foot in the New World. All this was achieved by a sophisticated method of information capture, allowing planners to interpret remote information and send codified drawings for builders to execute their designs. If we are looking for the origins of the Internet one might argue that architects, planners and builders had some say in the matter several hundred years ago. After all, the ability to transfer encoded information from one person to another over vast expanses of the world is a characteristic that is supposedly a new feature of the Internet. The evidence suggests otherwise. But what the Internet has brought about is a complete schism between thinking and doing – both geographically and over time. It is the realization of a process that has been underway for some time.

Every construction firm today is engaged in two worlds: a physical world of resources that managers can see and touch, and a virtual world made of information. The latter has given rise to what we call electronic commerce. Rayport and Sviokla (1995) describe these worlds as the *marketplace* and *marketspace*. Managers involved in construction must now deal with the creation of value in both of these worlds. However, the process of creating value in the two worlds is fundamentally different. Understanding the interplay of the marketplace and marketspace is a prerequisite to leveraging commercial advantage.

Virtual value chain

Having looked at a general framework to understand the nature of information, we have seen that the learning organization offers a radical way forward. Harnessing the Internet to produce learning organizations becomes the key challenge. But how do we develop Internet systems that bring commercial benefit to the construction firm – benefits that are sustainable and offer a long-term advantage in the marketplace? The reader may be familiar with the concept of supply chains. This refers to the sequence of interlinking supply activities involved with bringing a product to a consumer. The value chain concept is a more strategic way of looking at the progress of goods and services as they are transformed from a raw resource to a consumable resource. The value chain model is one that has proved effective in the manufacturing and construction industry. As a model it focuses on the process of creating value in the physical world, thinking of each value-adding step as a link in a value chain. In the realization of a completed building, we might think of the links as being the design, manufacture, supply, construction, commissioning and operation. The IMI Generic Design and Construction Process Protocol shown in Figure 2.1 illustrates the areas where value adding occurs (excluding off-site manufacture).

Superimposed on this are all the various internal value-adding steps in firms including supply side (raw materials, inbound logistics, and production processes) and demand side (outbound logistics, marketing and sales) activities.

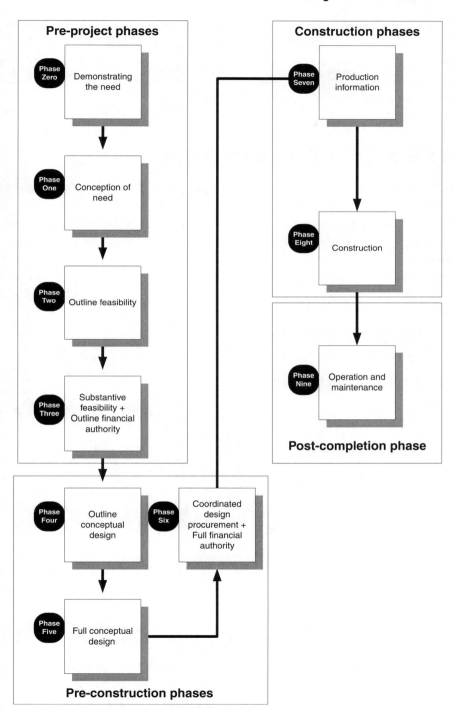

Fig. 2.1 EPSRC IMI Generic Design and Construction Process Protocol.

Rayport and Sviokla (1995) describe the emergence of the virtual value chain (VVC) that differs markedly from the conventional physical value chain (PVC) to which we usually refer in the context of value chains. In their research they found that successful companies were able to exploit both value chains. The two chains 'must be managed distinctly but also in concert'.

Three stages of virtual value adding

Value adding can be seen to occur in three distinct stages for organizations exploiting the Internet: (a) creating visibility, (b) mirroring activities and (c) creating new customer relationships. The first of these approaches uses Internet technology to make information less opaque and more transparent. This process of creating visibility provides a large-scale decision support system. It allows activities in the physical value chain to be coordinated (resourcing, scheduling, quality control and

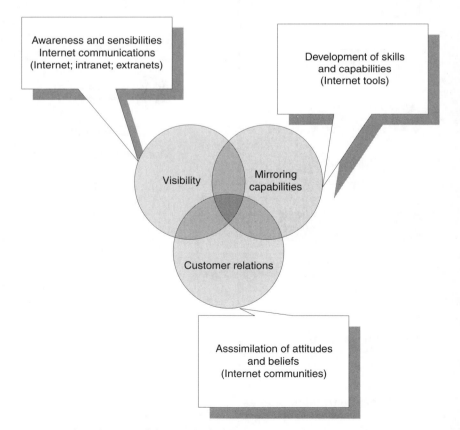

Fig. 2.2 Stages of development of the virtual value chain and its relationship with the deep learning cycle.

so forth). This paves the way for a second evolutionary stage in the formation of the virtual value chain. This involves mirroring activities previously undertaken in the physical value chain in the virtual value chain. During this stage of mirroring capabilities, the realm of activity moves from the marketplace to the marketspace. Finally, the information is used to create new customer relationships – the flow of information becomes a recognized part of a construction firm's offering to a client. Each of these evolutionary stages provides considerable opportunities for managers of design and construction firms. Figure 2.2 shows how this relates to our understanding of the deep learning cycle. Visibility is achieved by heightening awareness of information provided by various types of Internet infrastructure. Specialist capabilities, such as three-dimensional (3D) modelling, allow new capabilities previously only achievable as part of the physical value chain. Finally, the net technologies allow the assimilation of attitudes and beliefs of clients, using electronic communities. The following three chapters deal with each of these three stages in turn and the possibilities offered by each.

New economics of information

The schism between information and the physical value chain can be explained by a new phenomenon. This new phenomenon is not the result of any particular technology, but of a new mode of behaviour that is now reaching a critical mass. This behaviour involves the adoption of *open standards*. Standardization is bringing about an explosion in possibilities afforded by electronic networking and the Internet is the outward manifestation of it.

Many innovations in information technology have occurred in the construction industry since the early 1980s. Cost-estimating systems, CAD (computer-aided design) and EDI (electronic data interchange) have all acquired a place in firms' business processes. This has been achieved through a simple, although prolonged, process of adaptation. The new information technology revolution will require a much more fundamental rethink. Not an incremental change, but a fundamental change. Its effect will be felt throughout the entire construction industry – not just individual firms.

From physical to information resources

The construction industry has been insulated from the radical changes witnessed in the service sector up until now because informational components have remained locked into the physical value chain. Only once information components are able to acquire a separate existence can radical changes be achieved. This has meant that information has remained constrained by the linear flow of the physical value chain. This is why we use discrete segmented steps in the construction process – each bundled as separate contracts and delineated in time. The economics of information in this context becomes inextricably linked to the economics of things. However, the new wave of net technologies allows us to unbundle information from its physical carrier. As a result, we can expect to see a complete deconstruction of the value chain; a deconstruction of activities along entirely distinct value chains – the physical value chain and the virtual value chain.

Transformation of the economics of information

The economics of information (put forward by Coase, 1937 and Williamson, 1975) has been used to explain why (a) organizations are the size they are, (b) the point where markets become more effective than organizations, and (c) the form of communication that takes place within them. This whole theory on the economic exchange of information is governed by two competing factors, *richness* and *reach*, the argument being that you cannot have more of one without sacrificing the other. Richness refers to the quality of information. Reach refers to the number of people the information can be communicated to. Think of an electrical contractor trying to promote their business. They can choose to place an advert in a popular trade magazine, send out direct mail to a list of addresses, or make personal telephone calls to individual customers. An advertisement enables the contractor to reach a large audience, but the information is not targeted and there is no dialogue. At the other extreme, the telephone call provides a rich interactive channel for exchange, but only a limited number of people can be dealt with in this way.

What makes information rich? The three qualities of rich information are bandwidth, interactivity, and customization:

- *Bandwidth* refers to the volume of information that can be carried in a given time. Videoconferencing carried out over a local network is able to make use of a larger bandwidth than one requiring long distance communication, since dedicated cabling and short distances are involved. Physical proximity reduces the costs involved.
- *Interactivity* describes the ability for a two-way exchange of information. In the example of a telephone call, the customer is able to enquire further about the contractor's product and get the information they need.
- *Customization* describes the extent to which the information is tailored to the audience. By targeting the audience and refining the message based on an in-depth knowledge of the customer, a successful outcome is more likely.

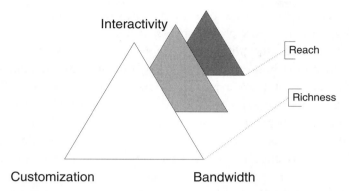

Interactivity

Reach

Richness

Customization   Bandwidth

Fig. 2.3 Trade-off between 'richness' and 'reach' in a traditional model of information economics.

Figure 2.3 shows the three facets of information richness.

The rules governing the economics of information are about to be redefined. The advent of open standards means that firms are no longer constrained by the trade-off between richness and reach. Rich information can be achieved using net technologies and communicated to a large and previously disconnected community. The

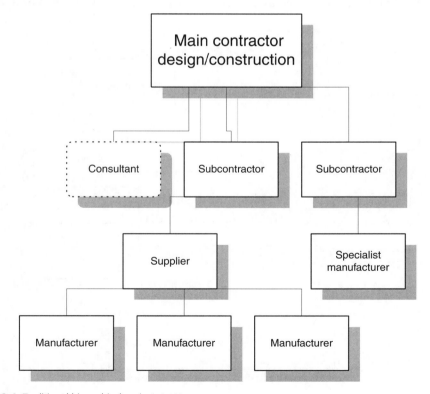

Main contractor design/construction

Consultant   Subcontractor   Subcontractor

Supplier   Specialist manufacturer

Manufacturer   Manufacturer   Manufacturer

Fig. 2.4 Traditional hierarchical project structure.

whole rationale for a firm's size and position in the value chain comes under scrutiny. The factors governing the size of the firm – *span* and *control* – are opened up. Firms have evolved as separate entities in the construction marketplace because they develop a system of rich information flow. The proximity and familiarity of people within the firm enables this exchange. Markets allow the flow of thinner information, but to a much larger external group. The transition of construction projects involves a continual alternation between rich and thin information flow as activities move from the firm to the marketplace. However, new Internet technologies allow both richness and reach. The transaction costs that have previously prevented exchange of rich information in the marketplace no longer exist.

Span and control no longer need to be achieved within the context of the rigid reporting system of a firm's hierarchy. Not only will the hierarchical structure of the firm be reworked, the hierarchical structure of the construction project will need to be reinvented. What are the effects of eliminating the trade-off between richness and reach? Figure 2.4 shows the prevailing structure of the construction project, dominated by rigid channels and a progression from main contractor, through subcontractors, suppliers and manufacturers. Figure 2.5 shows what Evans and Wurster (1997) describe as the hyperarchy (after the hyperlinks of the World Wide

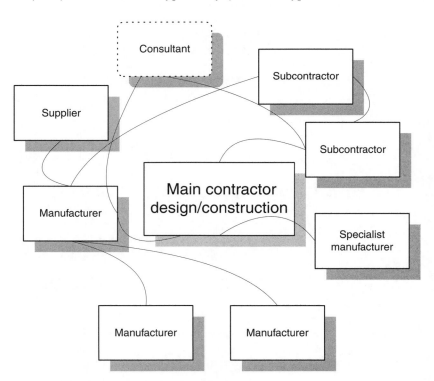

Fig. 2.5 Hyperarchy – deconstructed value chain of construction project.

Web). It shows how the value chain is being deconstructed, allowing specialist manufacturers and subcontractors to have much more direct influence on the design and construction process. The role of the main contractor is redefined as an enabler and monitor rather than an enforcer. Much more fluid team-based collaboration also emerges and conventional reporting structures are bypassed. For firms involved in construction, the hyperarchy provides a way to understand not only positioning strategies within the construction industry, but also more fundamental questions of size and identity.

Zero-sum game

How does the advent of the virtual value chain impact on your firm? Does it just mean that we will all have to work harder just to stand still? Exploiting the virtual value chain enables us to do more than simply improve performance. It also opens up avenues for creating a sustainable advantage, provided that our Internet strategy is based on sound reasoning.

> Constant improvement in operational effectiveness is necessary to achieve superior profitability. However it is not usually sufficient. Few companies have competed successfully on the basis of operational effectiveness over an extended period of time.

This provocative statement by Porter (1996) is particularly pertinent at this point in the book. Porter goes on to argue that 'operational effectiveness competition shifts the frontier outward, effectively raising the bar for everyone. But although such competition produces absolute improvement in operational effectiveness, it leads to relative improvement for no one.' Are all construction firms involved in a zero-sum game? Is this all the Internet is capable of offering – an improvement in operational efficiency with no sustainable advantage? The answer to this is a definitive no – what is required is a focus on strategic positioning. In this chapter we explore what form this might take.

Operational effectiveness (OE) is all about doing similar activities better than competitors. In the construction industry there are many hundreds of activities involved with creating, producing and selling a building. Cost arises from carrying out activities and cost advantage results from carrying out these activities more efficiently than competitors. We can say that activities form the basis of competitive advantage and it is the sum total of these activities that determines market advantage. In contrast to operational effectiveness, strategic positioning means performing different activities from rivals or performing similar activities in different ways.

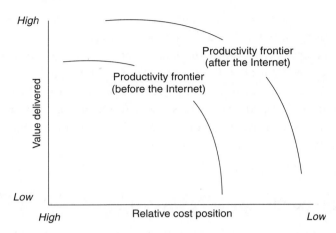

Fig. 2.6 Productivity frontier and the state of best practice.

The concept of operational effectiveness in relation to the Internet can be explored by the idea of the productivity frontier as shown in Figure 2.6. This is an imaginary barrier that represents the state of best practice. It constitutes the maximum value a company can deliver at a given cost, using the best available technologies. As a company improves its practices, it moves towards the productivity frontier. The advent of the Internet has substantially moved this productivity frontier. Other innovations, such as total quality management, benchmarking, concurrent engineering and value engineering, have further raised the limits of the productivity frontier.

The result of construction firms competing for operational efficiency is that major productivity gains are being captured not by producers, but by clients. Improvements are not reflected in profits. Another phenomenon that Porter describes as being more insidious is the process of 'competitive convergence'. The process of imitation (in construction technologies, management techniques, procurement techniques and information technology) creates a race down identical paths, with no winners. Companies become drawn into imitation and homogeneity.

A company can outperform rivals only if it can establish a difference that it can preserve. This process of creating a difference derives from *strategic positioning*. These are new positions that 'attract customers from established positions or draw new customers into the market' (Porter, 1996).

Internet strategy and fit

The learning organization emphasizes the primacy of the whole. It is not the effectiveness of individual activities that makes for a sustainable Internet advantage. Rather, it is strategy that focuses on how these individual activities are combined – how the whole system of activities interact. This is completely at odds with popular management views about core competencies and critical success factors. Understanding this holistic view is the key to Internet success. Part of this involves understanding the concept of *fit*. This concept of fit provides a way of locking out imitators by creating a chain that is 'as strong as its strongest link' (Porter, 1996). This applies to the physical and virtual value chain that we looked at in an earlier chapter. Fit is based on the affirmation that construction firms must make trade-offs. The existence of trade-offs is the reason why firms need strategies. Simple operational efficiency does not lead to trade-offs. Strategies do this by asserting what you intend *not* to do. Porter (1996) illustrates this point by examining the success of Southwest airlines that has achieved market leadership by reducing the turnaround time with its flights. This has been achieved by changes to a number of its seemingly unrelated activities. No meals are served on the flights, there are no seat assignments, no baggage transfers between flights. Routes are chosen that avoid congestion. Here we see no evidence of a core competence – rather a set of activities that are coherent, not an isolated set of parts.

How do we forge a fit between activities and how does the Internet relate to this process? There are three distinct types of fit. The first of these is *simple consistency*. A building firm pursuing a flexible, market-responsive strategy might emphasize flexible labour, the ability to hire rather than purchase equipment, and minimal investment in equipment, choosing to hire instead. This might be a strategy they have developed based on their perception of uncertainties and risks in their particular sector. Another firm may pursue a strategy that places emphasis on in-house learning, with a retained labour force, an established craft training programme and ownership of equipment to ensure availability of plant on site. Both of these are legitimate strategies – but there is no in-between. The strength in each strategy lies in their internal consistency.

Another form of fit is *reinforcing*. It revolves around the ability to kill two birds with one stone. By choosing to align with one particular construction sector or product, firms are able to rationalize their marketing effort. Their message is not diluted. Firms venturing into the facilities management of medical facilities are able to refine their understanding of the design of medical facilities. In this way they are able to acquire greater feedback and better design solutions. The last form of fit perhaps most relevant to the Internet is that of *optimization of effort*. Co-ordination and information exchange are not activities *per se*, but are the lubricating oil between activities. They enable the optimization of effort. Duplication of draughting activities can be eliminated by enforcing layering conventions when exchanging files with subcontractors. The implementation of standards can reduce the effort involved in payments using EDI.

To illustrate this idea of fit, an activity–system map can be used to highlight the interrelationships that exist within a coherent strategy. In Figure 2.7 we see an

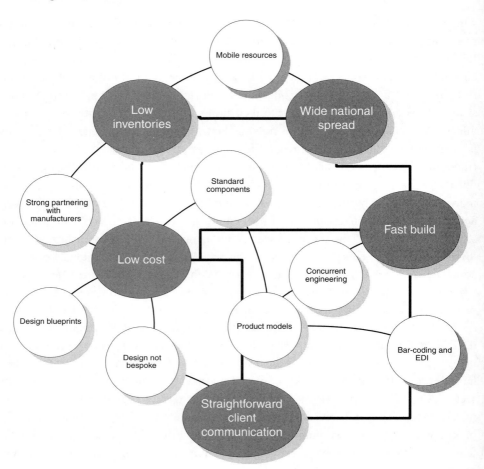

Fig. 2.7 Activity–systems map for a design-build firm specializing in factory units.

example of a strategy for a firm that specializes in factory warehouse buildings. Notice how their IT and Internet strategy is likely to gravitate towards object-modelling technologies because of the use of standard components for the particular market sector. Another firm might place greater emphasis on visualization, client dialogue through videoconferencing, and local intranet technologies provided via a local area network.

KEY POINTS FROM THIS CHAPTER

- The virtual value chain describes all the value-adding stages of an enterprise that are achieved through Internet technology.

- The virtual value chain must be managed distinctly from the physical value chain but in concert.

- The virtual value chain can involve creating visibility.

- The virtual value chain can involve mirroring capabilities previously undertaken through the physical value chain.

- The virtual value chain can involve the creation of new customer relationships.

- The Internet should enable firms to do more than simply push forward the efficiency frontier. Otherwise they will be the victims of *competitive convergence*.

- Construction firms should establish a sustainable advantage by taking a strategic position involving the Internet.

- An Internet strategy should involve the formulation of a strategic fit – either *simple consistency, reinforcing fit, or optimization of effort*.

3

Creating visibility

Questions addressed in this chapter

- Why embody knowledge?

- What type of Internet system will enable firms to capture knowledge?

- What are the differences between a static and a dynamic on-line information system?

- How are international construction firms making use of dynamic information?

- What developments in Internet open standards will enable semistructured information to be used as part of a corporate knowledge base?

The Internet gives managers the ability to *see* their value chain. For construction projects the ability to co-ordinate, measure and control are vital business processes. They allow cost managers to quickly evaluate the value of work done, they allow design managers to measure the progress of design, and they allow site managers to execute site activities. Feeding into this system is a complex system of data capture. The presence of an integrated system allows managers to see the project as a whole. Documents form a central part of this process. The first section of this book looks at the design, creation and management of such documents as part of this first evolutionary stage of visibility. We see that visibility requires much more than the creation of digital documents in cyberspace. It requires a new method of creation that has implications for everyone in a construction firm.

Visibility and the learning organization

In the construction industry much of the learning process can be described as experiential learning (Kolb, 1984). Individuals learn by doing. Looking at the amount of money spent on training and development in construction one is led to believe that 99% of learning takes place through doing. We often consider experiential learning not as learning at all but just as general experience. Experience in using a particular piece of plant or machinery on site, experience with a particular design solution, experience with a particular customer are all legitimate forms of learning. However, in many construction sectors this experience stops short at the individual or team level. No attempt is made to encode history, or to routinize experience in order to guide behaviour in subsequent projects. For the individual this is not a problem. They are able to carry their experience with them to other firms. Indeed, it is often the exclusivity of this experience which may make them attractive to another organization. The loser is invariably the organization itself, which allows the inevitable migration of know-how and experience without having a mechanism to embody this knowledge. The future of the construction organization thus depends on its ability to embody knowledge.

Static and dynamic information

With the advent of Internet technology a number of opportunities have developed which will facilitate the growth of a learning organization. A global network provides a mechanism for both distributing and integrating human intelligence. During the early evolution of the World Wide Web much criticism was pointed at the anarchic way in which information tended to mushroom. The flexibility of Web documents (using hypertext markup language (HTML)) also presented a problem, as there was no way of ordering information. For large organizations dealing with many thousands of standards, drawings and reports this represented a major limitation. This *static* method of information storage is now being superseded by a *dynamic* model whereby information is stored in databases. This means that the raw information is devoid of any markup information. Large records can be stored and managed as part of a larger body of information that can be searched by people and machines. Table 3.1 shows the contrasting natures of the static and dynamic models for encoding information on the Internet.

Web-enabled databases began to appear in the late 1990s with products such as Domino by Lotus and dBAnyware by Symantec. These software packages are able to act as middleware, funnelling information from a server's database to the client that is requesting the information. Using Web document (HTML) templates it is

Table 3.1 Static versus dynamic views of Web-based information

Static model	Dynamic model
Uses Web documents (HTML) for both storage and transfer to the user (user) on a network.	Uses a database for information storage, generating Web documents on-the-fly following a query by the user.
Needs to be created and maintained using Web authoring language (HTML).	Can be created and maintained as entry fields (forms) using a Web browser.
Generates information which is not readily searchable or structured.	Generates structured information which can be interrogated and analysed.
Creates information which rapidly becomes obsolete.	Creates information which can be easily updated.
Information must be maintained locally by Web author.	Information can be entered by the person with the information, avoiding any intermediaries, further increasing the timeliness of the information.

then possible to massage the database information into any form of document to be viewed on the World Wide Web. For the user, information does not appear as bland database records but as integrated information containing text, images, drawings and multimedia. More recently, the emergence of products such as Filemaker Pro and Microsoft Access using Active Server Pages has made on-the-fly database delivery an almost seamless process. What implications does this have for the learning organization in construction?

- It allows distributed databases to be used that encode learning in a structured way in a form that relates to the processes of the organization.
- It allows those teams or individuals who have acquired the experience to encode the learning instance themselves using remote password access (in contrast to unwieldy central databases of the past which were centrally administered and quickly became obsolete and uneconomic to maintain).
- It overcomes the costs associated with maintaining software and data at every workstation – this approach is known as *thin-client* architecture whereby only a minimal amount of processing occurs at the user's (client) end and much of the heavy processing and data storage occurs on a remote server.

If a user performs an operation such as a search or a simulation the request is transmitted to a remote server. The resulting output is then returned to the user as if the operation had been performed locally on their own PC. The financial savings resulting from this approach are immense. In principle it is possible to continue using PC workstations that would otherwise be rendered obsolete, because the processing power resides in the server. Instead of upgrading the PC, technological advances in hardware technology can be assimilated by new server technology. Another advantage of this approach is that system administration and software maintenance is undertaken at a central server. Employees are not embroiled in purchasing, software installation and configuration issues. This is perhaps one of the biggest hidden costs of IT in the service industries. The time which users invariably spend dealing with software maintenance issues has been estimated to run into about 10% of an employee's overall time. Translate this into hard financial sums and you soon realize the financial burden that IT is imposing on companies.

How are construction organizations attempting to embody knowledge? The case study that follows demonstrates the range of experiential knowledge that is being captured by one organization to bring about organizational learning on a global scale. The problems of regional variations in legal, contractual, cultural, resource and economic terms often prevent construction firms from operating globally. For this reason, many firms confine their operation to local areas, exploiting their knowledge of the regional operating environment. However, as the case study suggests, large organizations are able to sustain global operations in construction with the help of networking technology.

Bechtel Corporation

The Bechtel Corporation is one of the truly global organizations in construction. They undertake engineering and construction work in over 75 offices around the world and encompass more than 100 subsidiary companies. Their work ranges from consultancy to complete design-manage-build-and-operate (DMBO) contracts. Increasingly, they are seeking to undertake complete lump-sum turnkey projects which entail rolling several related projects into one larger operation. Standardization is a critical element of such projects. Through standardization, the benefits of IT integration and work process integration are able to follow through from one phase to another. For a corporation of this size it is possible to slice the pie in many ways but its geographical divisions fall into three key areas: the Americas; Europe, Asia and the Middle East (EAMS); and Asia Pacific. Operations are headed from their headquarters in Los Angeles, but levels of autonomy exist at each of the regional divisions.

From an information technology perspective, the pie cuts another way. The top tier, known as Information System & Technology, provides direct board-level influence, and is in turn split into several functional elements. The nature of this split is particularly revealing in terms of their consciousness of Internet potential. The elements include:

- regional (America, EAMS, Asia Pacific);
- collaborative work (which, to date, has become synonymous with Web development);
- infrastructure (which focuses on cabling and communications issues);

- software development (to support business processes);
- commercial development (to generate income from IT systems development).

What were the origins of Internet development within Bechtel? It appears that the first people to experiment with it were the Civils group in Houston around 1995. The Web quickly ballooned within the space of only a year. Like so many examples of Internet innovation, the ability of an organization to provide the freedom for experimentation is what set the touch paper alight. As with the development of the Internet in general, it was not the specialists in information technology but area specialists (in this case civil engineers) who have recognized the potential of the Internet.

Communications infrastructure

Bechtel currently uses a global wide area network (WAN). This network uses the TCP IP protocol (the computer communication language of the Internet) and is increasingly being used for Internet applications. The extent of the WAN is vast, linking offices as far afield as Al Khobar, Brisbane and Sao Paulo. The infrastructure forms an intricate network with bandwidths ranging from the very fast 1.5 Mb per second links in offices such as Gaithersburg in Sweden to the remote sites such as Buenos Aires with bandwidths as low as 64 kb per second. For some Internet applications requiring high bandwidth, such as video conferencing, the slower connections afforded by the more remote locations present difficulties. For these types of application the importance of guaranteed bandwidth availability is of paramount importance. The move towards an Internet (as opposed to an intranet) system will have to coincide with such a guarantee: developments in encryption technology and virtual private networks (VPNs) may enable this. The consequent savings derived from using the Internet instead of Bechtel's own proprietary global network may be considerable. Bechtel currently spend significant sums of money on line leases. The cabling infrastructure is not restricted to permanent offices but also extends to site offices. Every major construction site is connected via a high-speed leased line.

Bechtel have invested heavily in intranet development, seeing this as a mechanism to rapidly enable and expand communications within Bechtel and with external customers. The company is seeking to develop a thin-client environment whereby the user's workstation simply serves as a conduit or window to information that is stored and processed remotely by a server.

Structured information is stored on server databases which conform to the ODBC (object-database-compliant) standard. Many software applications support this standard, which allows cross-platform and cross-application transfer of database information. When used in a client–server environment it enables a variety of solutions to be used that are not tied to a single software vendor.

Bechtel's global knowledge network

As early as 1996 Bechtel began the corporate-wide roll-out of a Web-enabled system, providing a global knowledge network. The system, known as BecWeb, incorporates a globally adopted set of company standards for creating and communicating information across the Internet. It makes use of a number of existing legacy systems that were developed prior to the introduction of Web technology. These applications provided business interfaces in key areas of value delivery. The areas of application for the knowledge network BecWeb include:

- *Strategic marketing* – This part of BecWeb allows intelligence gathering based on real-time information covering different countries, competitors and market information.
- *Business development* – This covers profiles of customers, lead-times and product information. Sales teams operating in different countries or with different customers are able to share expertise and lessons learned.
- *Business management* – This part of the knowledge network is Internet based, providing pointers to external sources of Internet information covering development, economics, trade, currency and many other areas of relevance to the business.
- *Project development* – The diversity of countries in which Bechtel operate demands an in-depth knowledge of local laws. Using a network of regional law libraries covering local laws, development issues and conditions, Bechtel are in a strong position to forge relationships with local partners.
- *Global networking* – In many Internet applications, the location of the machine from which information is being retrieved remains relatively invisible. However, for the purposes of showing the *virtual* capability of an organization, it may be useful to highlight the geographical spread of a network. The global networking aspect of BecWeb is used to show the dynamics of global networking.
- *Estimating and procurement* – Worldwide information on suppliers, contractors, local labour markets and materials is maintained using BecWeb. This element of BecWeb is being developed to allow integration with suppliers. Suppliers are able to obtain technical specifications online.
- *Corporate services* – This aspect of BecWeb enables employees to access and transmit corporate information via the Web. Travel forms, time sheets and expense reports can be submitted using electronic forms. Human resource information such as corporate policies, company missions and goals, as well as job postings are made available through the system.

Underlying all of the BecWeb system is the opportunity for standardization across the organization. The immediacy of the Web allows single changes to be implemented instantaneously, without the need for continued replacement of hard-copy material such as manuals or standard forms.

Web implementation

Bechtel has had to tackle head-on the balance between empowerment and control. One of the greatest benefits of the Web is also one of its greatest shortcomings. For the first time it empowers individuals within an organization, with only a minimal knowledge of computing, to publish in any way they choose. Morever, it can tie up people's time at the expense of key business activities. Uncontrolled, this can soon lead to anarchy. A roll-out programme was initiated by Bechtel in 1997 to bring BecWeb into being. This involved the following phases:

- roll-out planning (includes the activities required to initiate full-scale development);
- team establishment;
- definition of roles and responsibilities;
- office participation;
- legacy migration and decomissioning;
- web-site prototyping;
- funding guidelines;
- definition of implementation schedule;
- development;
- management and support;
- web-site planning;
- web-site design and development;
- web-site implementation and maintenance.

The Web advisory board, responsible for putting together BecWeb, has had to develop a standardized approach for the roll-out of BecWeb, encompassing management support, employee training and policy documentation.

   The Bechtel case study shows how Internet technology can be used to embody knowledge within an organization. The use of Web-enabled database information provides a mechanism for codifying knowledge and distributing it throughout the organization.

Document-driven knowledge systems

Not all construction-based information can be maintained on a database. Much of the text-based semistructured material including contracts, manuals, procedures and specifications only exist as complete documents. In a later chapter we will look in more detail at new developments that enable the Internet to make use of this type of information in a much more sophisticated way.

Traditionally, the only way of dealing with semistructured information has been through the use of word-processed documents. But industries are now waking up to the possibility of using the document standard of the Internet (i.e. markup languages) in place of word-processed documents. This document format can be authored by everyone in the organization as a common text-based communication tool using low-cost editing devices. We will see how markup languages enable a quantum leap in the reuse of information because unambiguous meaning becomes more important than appearance and presentation.

Who needs machine interpretation?

So what is wrong with the ubiquitous word-processed document and all the templates and forms that construction organizations have standardized on? The ubiquitous word-processed document has served the needs of the industry for many years. But it has had its time. With its emphasis on display formats, it is designed to be human readable but not machine interpretable. Why should text be machine interpretable? In the creation of a contract document someone will have to write it and someone will have to read it. Are we suggesting that machines will displace humans, automatically generating a construction contract document and automatically validating a contract? Will machines be able to make use of the naive knowledge of the client to design complete building models, all without human intervention? This utopian view of computers is now seen as invalid. Only well-defined decision-making processes in construction can be carried out autonomously by computer systems. The bandwagon of *expert systems* evident in the 1980s has now been eclipsed by a different view of computers and their role. Expert systems rely on the existence of hard and fast rules. Such systems have proved very effective in specific, well-defined areas such as structural analysis. However, for much of the work in construction, rules are evasive. We rely on the essential intuitive thinking process of the construction professional. That is not to say that the construction professional is able to turn their back on computing systems. Rather, we need to redefine the role of computers as communication devices capable of transforming data into information. The primary role of networked computers is to provide *descriptive* rather than *prescriptive* information. The human sender and recipient remain the two most important agents in the process. Networked computers simply support the process, in a flexible evolutionary information environment, where hard rules are displaced by soft rules. The more features we incorporate into documents to allow computer interpretation, the greater the likelihood of obtaining meaningful results. Markup languages provide the flexibility to achieve this. Many other sectors, including the defence and medical industries, already recognize the benefits of using markup languages and require subcontractors to produce documentation based on markup standards.

Birth of markup languages

As early as the 1960s the Graphic Communications Association (GCA) and IBM implemented structured documents in a standard open format. IBM developed the generalized markup language (GML) to enable the management of documents of all types, from project specifications and contracts to manuals and press releases. This system was designed with a simple syntax to enable typists to mark-up documents, most of which involved the use of tagsets denoted by $< >$ and $< / >$. Information contained within these tags conveyed specific information about the structure of the document. However, a common problem was that typists would tend to minimize on the inclusion of markup within the documents, emphasis being placed on ease of typing and reading rather than the general purpose processing by computers. Parsing also formed part of the document-creation process. This term refers to preprocessing that a document undergoes before being published. This enabled information to be reusable so that books, reports and electronic editions could be produced from the same source file.

As the number of document types began to flourish, so did the need for different tagsets for use in markup. This soon led to the emergence of the document type definition or DTD. For each document type (e.g. a contract or a manual) a collection of appropriate tagsets were defined and expressed. These tagsets were embodied in a DTD which provides a machine-interpretable definition of a document type. The DTDs themselves became the subject of standardization. In the early 1980s representatives from the GML community got together to produce a standard markup language known as the standard generalized markup language (SGML) which was published as ISO Standard 8879 in 1986.

Some of the powerful characteristics of SGML include:

- *Reusability* – The parsing (preprocessing) process allows one document to be presented and reused in many different ways. The order and content of the resulting publication can be tailored to a particular user type or function. For example, an executive summary can be extracted from a collation of various parts.
- *Extensibility* – Authors can define new tagsets for documents by the specification of syntax (order in which something appears) and semantics (unambiguous definition of a term). For the construction process this enables tagsets (DTDs) to be created for particular processes (e.g. electronic data interchange) and for these to be modified incrementally over time.
- *Structure* – Documents can be containers for other documents, with an indefinite amount of nesting. Thus, for example, a master contract document can contain numerous nested clauses that are reused in various ways. Furthermore, these nested documents may bring with them their own DTDs. These might for example be definitions appropriate to a particular manufacturer's product specification.

- *Validation* – The use of a referenced grammar and vocabulary means that applications can validate documents, ensuring that they conform to a specific structure. Taking this idea further, we see that a document such as a quality assurance document for a steel specification becomes something between a conventional text document and a computer program. The absence of particular data in the document is highlighted in the parsing (preprocessing stage) forcing the user to add the missing information. In this example it might be tensile test data required as part of a quality assurance standard.

Web-based markup

By the late 1980s SGML was being adopted by organizations such as CERN (European Laboratory for Particle Physics in Switzerland). A research scientist called Tim Berners-Lee at CERN decided to develop a very small subset of the SGML standard. This subset involved the use of hypertext tags, enabling document readers to switch at will between different parts of documents, between different documents on the same machine and, most importantly, to skip between documents anywhere on the Internet. This was a dramatic development, because it enabled vast amounts of information to be knitted together in a manner that was easily accessible to people who were not computer programmers. The markup subset, called hypertext markup language (HTML) was released in 1990 and has since undergone a rapid adoption. This has been in tandem with the further refinement of programs capable of interpreting HTML documents (Web browsers). However, despite its networking virtues, HTML does not benefit from three of SGML's key attributes mentioned previously: extensibility, structure, and validation.

In the period since its development, further efforts have been made to formalize the HTML subset so that it rigorously conforms to SGML. This should enable proper unification between SGML and Web technologies.

The overall effect of using HTML is to migrate from a focus on *content* as separate from *presentation*. Word-processed documents accommodate this separation in a minimal way (e.g. style sheets) but the tendency is to encode presentational information (e.g. bold, italic) intractably within the document. The result is a much less flexible document that lends itself to only one rendition. In addition to its flexibility, HTML's hypertext, networking and open nature is likely to make it the preferred authoring environment of the future.

Arrival of XML

The three features of SGML – scalability, extensibility and structure – are three features that are absent from HTML. However, SGML is a standard that runs for

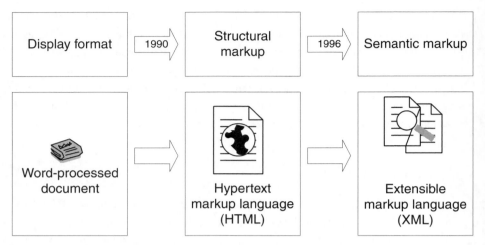

Fig. 3.1 Moving from presentation to semantics.

over 500 pages. Not only is the specification long, making it difficult for people to read and understand, it remains hard for computers to process and manipulate. In 1996 efforts were made to produce a standardized text format that would be easier to transfer over the Web. Moreover, it was the intention to produce a much more compact form of SGML that was easier to define, author and validate. This has given rise to a standard known as extensible markup language (XML) which occupies only 26 pages of specification. Figure 3.1 shows the likely evolution of document types with the advent of the Internet.

Some of the features that make XML an important language for the construction industry include:

- The compact nature makes it ideal for use on networks.
- The unambiguous nature of XML means that a well-formed document is interpretable by any SGML browser or editor. By reading the tags, it is possible to derive a complete hierarchical structure of the document, even without a DTD.
- As a subset of SGML, the translation from SGML to XML is straightforward.
- HTML documents can easily be migrated to XML with suitable semantic markup (i.e. labelling elements to indicate *meaning*).
- Unlike HTML, the linking model is more flexible. The new linking methods allow bidirectional and multidirectional linking (compared to single unidirectional linking with HTML).

Any organization involved in construction can define a simplified tagset appropriate to its needs. Furthermore, these DTDs can be brought together from simple DTDs to create more complex assemblages, capable of validation.

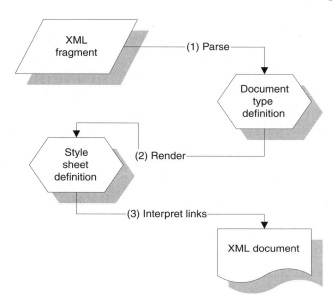

Fig. 3.2 Unpacking an XML document.

Templates and standard forms have been a prized possession of many construction organizations in the past. They have evolved internally to provide very effective methods for creating and issuing organizational know-how. In the future we can expect to see organizations investing substantial effort in the development of in-house DTDs to mark up their documents. These in turn may combine with project-wide DTDs, partnering DTDs, national and international DTD standards in the particular area of design or construction. The capacity to combine DTDs means that organizations are able to retain strategic in-house standards while being part of an industry-wide standard.

Figure 3.2 shows how a Web client (browser) receives and translates information transmitted as XML. The information is transferred as an XML fragment that is associated with a context wrapper, including an associated DTD and a specified style sheet (this defines the presentational style to be applied to the document). Using this context wrapping, a client browser is able to unwrap the information, by a sequential process of parsing (preprocessing), rendering, and finally the incorporation of hypertext linkages.

Overcoming information overload

The sudden growth of intranets in organizations is proof of the success of markup languages. Although intranets rely on secure private networks instead of the Internet proper, they do make use of tools and communication standards that have evolved in the open environment of the Internet. An intranet remains as a private entity, but organizations are able to enjoy low-cost authoring and browsing systems to communicate and receive information.

Construction professionals often complain about information overload. Not only does a single construction project give rise to many drawings – it also results in many text documents in all sorts of shapes and sizes. The accessibility of the World Wide Web is seen by many as a further overload on an already overburdened information system. So why advocate an information environment that is cluttered by irrelevant and unsubstantiated material? Well, largely because it is about to be reinvented in a form that is much more suited to the commercial environment. Visibility will be achieved by XML that will rejuvenate legacy documents and allow the reuse of material on a scale never experienced before.

KEY POINTS FROM THIS CHAPTER

- The future of construction firms depends on their ability to embody knowledge.

- The creation of on-line information enables firms' processes to become more visible to project partners and employees.

- Leading construction firms are deploying programmed roll-outs of intranet systems to enable their organizations to span cross-cultural divides.

- The use of on-the-fly technology is enabling firms to acquire and disseminate information to the people involved. The removal of intermediary personnel in this process will make information more reliable and more timely.

- Developments in markup languages will enable firms to develop embodied knowledge bases that are much more transportable – across platforms, software generations and across space.

- The Internet will not only influence our ability to transport information at the macro level, it will also dictate the way we store information at the micro level.

4

Creating new services

Questions addressed in this chapter

- Will the Internet give rise to new products and services in the construction industry?

- How will the design profession benefit?

- What new form will the design process take and what new specialists will be involved?

- What new forms of electronic communication will enable the substitution of face-to-face communication?

- How are organizations exploring the possibilities for new products and services in the construction industry today?

Mirroring capabilities

The Internet can be used to do more than simply monitor the existing physical value-added chain in construction. It can be used to manage operations and allows things to be done in the marketspace that could previously only be done in the marketplace. Products and services, previously delivered through the physical value chain, can exist as digital information and be delivered through information-based channels. This progression to the virtual value chain not only mirrors, but improves the value step. One example is the modelling of buildings. Previously this was undertaken using an arcane and labour-intensive craft involving materials such as card and glue. Today this has been largely supplanted by a marketspace offering of digital mock-ups.

These virtual reality mock-ups not only allow visual evaluation, but can also be the subject of thermal, structural, lighting and user behaviour simulations.

Another example of mirroring capabilities is the creation of virtual teams to supplant conventional design or construction project teams reliant on physical meetings. Global access means that the pool of professionals involved can be greatly extended – foundations experts; seismic experts, and microclimate experts can all become part of the team. This chapter explores how Internet technology is enabling things previously only possible in the marketplace to be undertaken in the marketspace.

We begin by looking at one area that will be keenly affected by the creation of new services, the design industry. Computer-aided design and its successor, the object-modelling environment, will give rise to many new services previously tied to the physical value chain. A whole new value chain is being created including simulation, visualization, prototyping, and specification using these technologies. Developments in the Internet environment will provide collaborative tools that will allow these technologies to be used concurrently and instantaneously over the Web.

Internet-enabled design

In the 1970s and 1980s CAD technology promised tremendous productivity and quality gains. Designers would no longer produce islands of information captured on paper. Instead, it was thought, digital information would be entered only once and shared seamlessly with others. In reality, what arose was very different from what was promised. CAD systems produced marginal benefits for many organizations over conventional drawing methods. This was because the electronic design invariably became committed to a hardcopy version at numerous stages. The electronic version was dispensed with and, at each stage, the drawing had to be recreated from scratch. This state of affairs helped to create an industry that was in the business of creating drawings rather than creating buildings. Difficulties with transferring electronic files between differing systems and concerns about intellectual property brought this about. However, many clients and construction firms today have addressed this problem. Methods have been established to allow CAD drawings to be transferred between heterogeneous platforms and applications. Issues of intellectual property and measurement of effort have been tackled. Clients are beginning to reap the benefits in terms of better quality control and lower costs. Contractors are able to get on with what they are best at – creating buildings.

Two developments will bring about unprecedented changes in CAD in the construction industry in the coming decade. The two technologies will combine to produce a step change in the design process. The first of these is the Internet-enabled CAD environment. The second is object modelling. The principles of object modelling rein-force and augment a network-enabled design environment. In the following sections we look beyond the issue of network enabling. We look at a system of design based on rich information – using object models.

Internet-enabled CAD

The mid-1990s saw the advent of the CAD browser. We are already familiar with the idea of a Web browser – a piece of versatile software that allows users to have a window on the world of the Internet. The CAD browser is a variation on this concept but, instead of using a text-based environment, CAD browsers use graphical representations as the primary means of communication. Drawing details appearing on a screen in front of the CAD designer may have been pulled from anywhere on the Internet. Networked CAD environments predate Internet-enabled CAD environ-ments by several years. Organizations such as the Building Design Partnership (BDP) in London, have developed in-house systems for co-authoring on local area networks (LANs). Such systems have drawn on various management tools to help with access control, authoring control and versioning. In such a networked environ-ment, parts of a drawing will undergo changes in the designer's absence, so that the next time a drawing is opened up more work will have been done on the design. Instead of dealing with a static portrayal, the drawing becomes a dynamic living entity – not a record.

The Internet-enabled CAD environment promises to integrate activities across projects and throughout product lifecycles. It represents a further extension of the networked CAD environment. Being an open system in terms of network accessibil-ity, software solution and platform independence, it allows many organizations in a project to engage in collaborative working. What is the marketplace for the Internet enabled CAD environment? Regli (1997) identifies five key players who will be instru-mental in the development of these systems: (1) software developers, (2) information authors, (3) information managers, (4) content providers and (5) service providers (Figure 4.1).

- *Software providers* – These organizations build the CAD systems or third-party applications that enhance a CAD system (e.g. facilities management third-party add-on to work with Intergraph). They will be responsible for creating the tools to allow interoperability over the Internet. This will involve the creation of intelligent programming interfaces and development environments for integrated network environments. To some extent, the idea of interoperability is at odds with the objectives of software providers. Interoperability encourages choice. Software developers wish to promote loyalty to a specific product. The

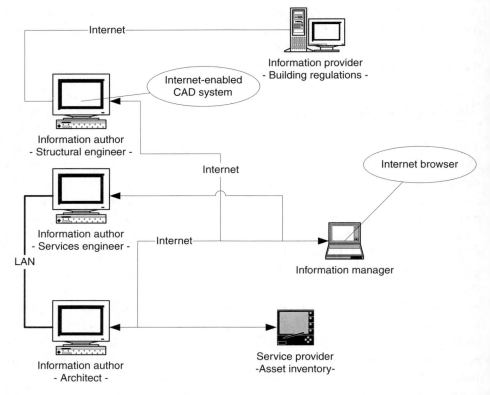

Fig. 4.1 Illustration of CAD infrastructure involving different providers and users (based on Regli, 1997).

very uniqueness of a software developer's offering may conflict with the idea of interoperability. The middle ground is the development of programming interfaces that allow some of the details of a software solution to be revealed.

- *Information authors* – These constitute the high-end users of CAD systems, making use of sophisticated product data management (PDM) tools. They continuously engage in the production of CAD drawings for information consumers. They also have to scan the considerable amount of on-line design information relevant to their tasks. Internet-aware CAD systems will provide the main interface to the Internet for such users.
- *Information managers* – Unlike information authors, information managers require only inexpensive user-friendly tools for accessing and marking up drawings. The manager makes decisions based on this information and passes on comments to various specialists. The tools required need only a high-level representation of the design data. This low-cost market is one that has supplanted

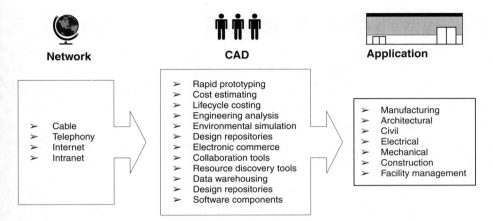

Fig. 4.2 Three levels of design infrastructure and the new engineering services (based on Regli, 1997).

a previous requirement for further costly workstations to view such information. *Internet browsers* provide an ideal candidate for this function.

- *Content providers* – Many content providers who have already used established media such as CD-ROM to distribute information to designers are turning to the Internet as a distribution medium. Content providers include public bodies responsible for issuing building standards, information on land ownership and planning, health and safety, and environmental assessment. Commercial organizations providing information on demographic information, cost estimates and indices, and design templates are able to elicit income on a per usage basis on the Internet. Manufacturers are able to increase the value-added elements of their products and make their products more visible and amenable to the designer via the Internet. Using the Internet, manufacturers are able to provide more than a description of their product – they are able to issue complete electronic models that can be accommodated instantaneously in a designer's drawing.

- *Service and information providers* – This new breed of construction professional will merge the applications domain of the construction industry with the network domain of the Internet. Figure 4.2 illustrates the intermediary role of the *service and information provider*. The network domain represents the lowest level of the design infrastructure, formed around telecommunications hardware, routers and fibre optics. The newly emerging service providers will lie one level above this and will increasingly satisfy the needs of various application sectors, including all the professional disciplines involved in construction process. Their role will be to develop agents, web sites and distributed software tools that enable CAD users to explore the Internet more effectively.

CAD browsers

CAD software developers rely upon the sale of licences to mainstream CAD users. Information managers, who require only a limited part of the functionality provided by a CAD system, are reluctant to pay for the privilege of a largely unused system. Software developers are thus developing cut-down compact versions for information users. The rationale behind this is that it adds value to the CAD author's offering, by enabling rapid dissemination. The performance requirements of these CAD browsers include:

- Viewing, printing and interrogation capabilities, providing access to a variety of native and neutral data formats. Data would include industry formats such as Autodesk's .dxf and .dwg standard and neutral standards such as the STEP AP203 standard (the STEP AP203 standard is the exchange standard for the boundary representation of solid models of mechanical artefacts and assemblies).
- Red-lining and markup facilities, allowing managers to make annotations regarding design features without affecting the original drawing.
- Hyperlinking capabilities allowing drawing components to be attached to hot-linkable addresses on the Internet. Linked information may include various views and locations within the CAD model itself as well as links to regulatory information and product catalogues.
- Limited translation capabilities allowing conversion to standard formats such as virtual reality markup language (VRML).
- Data filtering capabilities. The vast size of many CAD drawings imposes a considerable load on Internet traffic, with all of the associated download time penalties. As the information manager requires only high-level views of information, data filtering offers a way of considerably reducing file size.
- Portability across multiple platforms. In multidisciplinary projects involving many organizations, numerous types of computer platform are likely to be in use, from low-end Windows™ users to high-end Silicon Graphics™ users. For this reason, the CAD browsers should be usable on each of these platforms.

Existing CAD browsers

Whip – an Autodesk plug-in for Netsape Navigator – received considerable interest following its release in 1997. Its release coincided with the development of a new file format – a sibling of its standard .dwg format. The new .dwf format was designed specifically for Internet operation. It uses a highly compressed form of the parent file format. This is made possible by the elimination of numerous information about geometry and topology not required for high-level viewing. Compression levels with this format enable file sizes to be reduced by a factor of 10. Furthermore, the reliance on two-dimensional (2D) views, protects the intellectual property of companies releasing the drawings, as underlying information is not accessible. The Whip plug-in allows users to view both the standard .dwg and the compressed .dwf format. Features of the plug-in include zooming, layer selection, object manipulation and hyperlinking.

Another plug-in worthy of mention is InterCAP Graphics Systems' (a subsidiary of Intergraph) free CGM plug-in. This has many of the characteristics of the Whip plug-in but is designed to view industry standard Computer Graphics Metafiles (CGM). An additional feature of the CGM plug-in is the ability to red-line files. This is a feature of particular use to the information manager needing to mark up and comment on a designer's proposal.

Internet aware CAD data

CAD browsers serve only as viewing vehicles. In contrast, Internet-aware CAD systems are primarily design tools, but with the added feature of Internet intelligence. Any drawing element can have a hypertext address attached to it. These references enable geometric entities to be associated with many different views, rendered images and photographs. Furthermore, with Internet access, links can be encoded to various external sources. Examples include external hypertext documents explaining the designer's intent – a feature often criticized as being absent in traditional CAD models. Other organizations can also be linked to within a single drawing model – producing a virtual corporation. An example of this is the design of the Buffalo International Airport. In this project Microstation Link was used to produce a virtual corporation comprising the architectural firm, contractors, and the city, state and airport officials. This information-rich model demonstrates a perspective of the CAD model dramatically different from the geometry-centred environment we are so accustomed to.

Hyperlinking is a feature present in many of the high-end CAD systems – but these rely on their own internal addressing system. The argument for this is that it provides greater rigour over the content structure of cross-referenced material than loosely defined Internet addresses. However, for multiparty construction projects, a proprietary system tightly defined in this way is likely to have limited extensibility. A middle-ground solution appears to be the incorporation of Web-enabled PDM systems. An example of this is MetaWeb from Structural Dynamics Research Corporation (SDRC). Using MetaWeb as the Netscape Navigator interface, users can browse the complete set of product data. Further efforts are being made within the system to create an object server that integrates heterogeneous sources such as CAD and computer-aided manufacturing.

Shortcomings of CAD

Even the ability to structure CAD documents using hypertext links does not overcome the fact that CAD data is essentially *lean* in nature. Structure is only introduced into CAD models as an *ex post* activity. Geometric shapes are grouped, linked and annotated as a secondary process. Various attempts have been made to impose greater constraints on the way CAD models are generated. Examples include layering conventions. However, the extent to which individual drawings conform to these standards remains subject to the whims and idiosyncracies of the individual CAD designer. A common outcome is an electronic drawing that is capable of being migrated to another contractor's design team in a form that is so noncontiguous with the receiving contractor's method of drawing that much of the information is useless. Only by a very labour-intensive process can this information be assimilated by the new user.

Typically, CAD uses lines, circles and numerous other geometric shapes to represent a design element. As such, the information is simply a reproduction of the drawing-board model that it replaced. A detail of a section through a curtain walling system is produced by a large array of lines and segments, grouped together to give the impression of a coherent representation. The limitations of this system soon arise when the designer wants to do one of the following:

- represent the curtain wall detail at a different scale (e.g. zooming in). In order to do this the designer has to reproduce the drawing with different line weights, different detail inclusions and text labels;
- present different elevations or sections of the curtain walling system. Only by redrawing each of the various views is it possible to represent the 3D characteristics of the curtain walling system;
- obtain information about an element of the curtain wall. In CAD systems, information is added after the element is drawn. It is a separate and optional activity that rarely results in adequate information being incorporated in the drawing. With the object modelling approach information goes with the drawn element as an inextricable part of the process. The designer creates a part, such as a window frame, by explicitly choosing it from a product model. Not only do the lines appear on the screen, but all the information baggage that goes with it. This might include the dimensions, material properties, strength characteristics or cost details.

Object modelling

Object modelling provides a radical step away from the disorganization of conventional CAD. Most leading CAD developers are now providing a migration path away from *lean* CAD models to these sophisticated object-based systems. A key characteristic of object models is the use of *inheritance*. Any design is composed of a plethora of systems and objects. In principle, it is possible to disaggregate a design entirely into discrete components or objects. Typically, these objects may possess unique characteristics (e.g. a bespoke door frame), but are likely to have something in common with a much wider class of object found in many different designs, for example, a steel lintel of type X manufactured by Company Z. Unlike the traditional CAD approach, where this discrete object is created from scratch, using object technology the designer simply has to identify the class of object which their design component comes from. In this way, the component *inherits* characteristics common to a particular class of object. This definition may be related to a very wide class of components (e.g. fire resistant circulation doors) or a much more specific class (e.g. product X). Once an object is defined, it is possible to associate a complete package of information that goes with it. Information might include dimensions, costs, assembly order, strength characteristics and so forth. As the designer has pulled the object from a previously created catalogue of objects, there is no data entry overhead imposed on the designer to create this package. Furthermore, the design becomes much more than a collection of geometric objects from which the viewer must infer information. Instead, it becomes a detailed representation that can be presented in many different ways to meet the information requirement of numerous professionals. The model can rapidly produce a complete set of costs from an analysis of the objects. The same model might also provide a rendered view for an interior designer or a detailed specification for use by a subcontractor.

Of course designs are not just a collection of discrete items – their effectiveness relies on the interrelationship between the various elements. Object models allow the designer to define these relationships explicitly. How is a ducting system suspended from a ceiling? How does a window detail co-ordinate with a curtain walling system? By introducing relationships between objects the designer can begin to explore its behavioural characteristics. The model can be made to conform to the physical laws we know apply in the real world – laws of motion, thermodynamics, forces, light and so forth. Much of the information required to simulate how our design performs is already carried in the objects' information packages. By testing the model we are able to find out whether objects are going to end up sharing the same space (clash detection); whether structural systems are likely to fail; or whether lighting systems will produce glare at the workplace. Objects can also acquire motion characteristics so we can reproduce the behaviour of buildings subject to oscillations in earthquakes, or examine the wear characteristics of mechanical plant.

The migration to object modelling is not without difficulties. Clearly, the drawing process becomes fundamentally different. The designer may have to spend more time creating the initial drawing (model). This can be justified by the downstream benefits associated with information 'richness' and ease of modification. Many other users will be able to elicit information from the drawing. However, the designers' role becomes much more than simply communicating the next stage in the process. They are drawing something that will form the foundations of a complete system analysis. How does this 'fit' with the principal role of the designer as 'idea generator' and creator? Does modelling impose a frame of mind that conflicts with this creative process? These questions are having to be dealt with by many construction firms. Perhaps the most responsive disciplines to the idea of object modelling are the building services professions. This is perhaps no surprise, given that system analysis forms an integral part of the designer's role. For the architectural professions though, the switch to an object-modelling environment is less straightforward. However, the more transparent the object-modelling process becomes the less of a barrier it is likely to present to the designer. Access to more comprehensive object model libraries is likely to help with this process. The burden of defining bespoke object model libraries is likely to defeat the main benefit of object modelling – that of productivity improvements. A major challenge therefore is the definition and creation of electronic objects for use in construction.

Another hurdle to overcome in construction is the absence of component standards. A strong antipathy exists in many countries and construction sectors to standardization. Quality equals bespokeness. The more ornate and idiosyncratic a design, the more suited it is to the needs of the client. Many contractors are now questioning the wisdom of this approach. Although individuality is something that many clients seek, this does not need to interfere with many of the nonaesthetic characteristics of a design such as window mullion widths, window frame sizes or duct sizes. The concept of object modelling depends on the idea of standardization at a certain level. In manufacturing, standardization is a key part of the recipe for productivity. However, this does not preclude tailored and differentiated offerings. For the construction process, not only does nonstandardization increase production costs, it also presents difficulties for the object-modelling designer. Nonstandard components have to be newly created as object models. One feature of object modelling that may reduce this problem is the concept of *parameterization*. To explain this concept, consider a designer specifying a window unit. Given the freedom to specify a window of any size the designer may choose a width of, say, 1.2 metres. Having stipulated this value, the object incorporated into the model is one with a single glazing unit. However, on reviewing this value and changing it to a value of 2 metres, the object-modelling system creates an object that contains two glazing units to span the length, with an intervening partition. The software is incorporating a level of artificial intelligence, guiding the designer in the choice of objects, based on rules pertaining to the design of windows. This approach uses parameterization, whereby the designer defines not the object itself but the dimensional units necessary to choose the object. The subsequent selection is undertaken by the application of expert rules. This idea again raises many questions. Flexibility is not always a good thing – yes, a designer can specify a non-standard door width, but what are the additional fabrication costs or replacement costs? Parameterization, intelligent design rules and limited object sets may help to constrain the choice of design solutions – with the intent of increasing the quality of designs.

Object modelling standards

One great thing about standards is that there are so many to choose from. (anon)

For the senior managers of construction firms, there is perhaps nothing more disconcerting about the language of IT than the various acronyms and standards that abound – standards that appear to come and go, development efforts wasted and test-beds shelved. However, in the area of object modelling, there are a few standards of particular importance and likely longevity – standards that will enable object models to operate over the Internet.

Object linking and embedding for design and modelling

Object linking and embedding (OLE) for design and modelling is an industry-led initiative to produce an automated interface for geometric modelling and CAD systems. It involves leading developers, including Intergraph, Autodesk, and Bentley – who have incorporated OLE technology in their products. These systems enable features such as 'dragging and dropping' between applications and tight integration between CAD and various analysis tools. Although primarily a Windows^{TM}-based system, OLE is also being incorporated on Unix and Macintosh platforms. In facilities management programs it is frequently used as a method for integrating database information with CAD systems, as with inventory management. Other obvious areas are the use of VisualBasic^{TM} to allow the integration of CAD models and cost models in spreadsheets. OLE is likely to receive a further boost in the context of Internet application with the advent of the distributed common object model (DCOM). This will enable interfaces to be accessible using Internet protocols.

Common object request broker architecture (CORBA)

In contrast to OLE, which is a platform-dependent environment designed primarily for single users, CORBA is designed for distributed object systems – and is more pertinent to Internet development. CORBA is being used to develop application integration frameworks for particular industries such as finance, healthcare and manufacturing. These frameworks involve the combination of CORBA-specified services with user-specified applications. Various tools are helping developers to quickly write and deliver CORBA-based systems that act on an enterprise-wide basis. An example is Netscape's ONE (Open Network Environment) which incorporates an open standard for distributing software objects.

Java

The Java language, developed by Sun Systems, is a particularly exciting open standard that is likely to complement the role of CORBA. It is designed to operate as a programming tool for producing platform-independent tools, systems and agents. Java represents a next-generation programming language that will radically alter the face of distributed Internet programming. In its current form Java does not present a viable alternative for complete CAD systems. However, it is ideal as an intermediary environment. Users will be able to load Java-based objects and link them together to produce powerful tools. Unlike CORBA and OLE, there are no established libraries in Java to support solid and geometric modelling. Inevitably, given the inertia and legacy of systems tied to existing CAD products, Java is unlikely to displace these systems overnight. However, Java is already an established element of commercial CAD products. Increasingly we can expect to see (a) greater accessibility to CAD subsystems over the Internet using Java and (b) greater network-based programming opportunities using Java.

Data protocols

So far we have looked at technologies and standards that allow integration of systems over networks. However, in the context of object models we are still left with the problem of defining objects – exactly what package of information should accompany an object and in what format? Various object-modelling systems have been used by construction firms in the 1990s – but all have been dependent on the software developer or user creating a suitable object-model library. For complex building designs this becomes a mammoth undertaking. The problem of defining objects is not unique to the construction industry. STEP is an ISO standard (10303, 1995) that arose as a result of mutiple-industry collaboration to address exactly this problem. It provides a standard for exchanging product model data. It applies protocols prescribing the information requirements to perform specific activities (one example being configuration controlled 3D design). Particular industries instrumental in formulating the STEP standards are the aerospace and healthcare industries.

Creating the industrial virtual enterprise

With the emergence of the Internet, the STEP standard has moved to centre stage. Why should this be? The STEP initiative was instigated in the early 1990s at a time when the significance of the Internet was far from evident. Now organizations are beginning to talk of the industrial virtual enterprise (IVE). Such enterprises should be able to produce a seamless conduit of information flow between contractors, clients and consultants via the Internet. The current situation is far from seamless – data produced by the systems in one organization cannot be read by those at another. The construction industry is at a watershed in time – is the prospect of an IVE a practical possibility in the near future? Evidence from other industries suggests that the concept of IVEs is not too far away.

Hardwick and Spooner (1997) describe a demonstration project initiated by the National Industrial Information Infrastructure Protocols (NIIIP) Consortium to prove the possibilities of IVEs. It is worth examining at this juncture how the demonstration project exploited the STEP standard for the purposes of the organizations involved. Enterprises involved in the project included Boeing, General Electric, Rolls Royce and Pratt and Whitney. The first phase of this work involved three protocols designed to allow Internet access to industrial product data using the STEP standard. In the demonstration system, the component assembly required to produce an aircraft skin was modelled on an Internet server. Product information included assembly cost information applied as part of the AP203 STEP standard.

However, STEP was not the only option available for the demonstration project. Other neutral standards for exchanging model data were also considered, including VRML and Initial Graphics Exchange Standard (IGES), but neither contained the necessary product assembly information required for the cost-modelling exercise being used in their modelling scenario. Another alternative was to apply a single, integrated system for managing IVE data. This would bypass the need for any exchange processes at all, because everyone involved in the value chain would be using the same system. The main contractor would provide access to the model via a set of Internet interfaces. One clear benefit of this approach is that it avoids accuracy problems that inevitably arise as a result of translation between different systems. Despite the initial appeal of this solution it is flawed in two ways:

1. It does not provide a solution for projects involving more than one prime contractor.
2. It requires the supply chain to use the prime contractor's integrated system to create data.

Intellectual property and reliance on proprietary systems are directly challenged in such a scenario. There are many examples of subcontractors in construction industry projects investing large sums of money on integration initiatives that have served only the requirements of the particular project. One example is the investment in hardware systems including costly routers to support the Bluewater shopping centre project in the UK – contractors were concerned that much of this infrastructure would be of little use in subsequent projects that would invariably use a different protocol.

Sharing STEP data across CAD systems

The first part of the NIIIP demonstration project sought to demonstrate the technical feasibility of using several different CAD databases to exchange CAD files. Figure 4.3 shows the network design of the system. Underlying this apparently simple model, three protocol levels were required to make STEP function over the Internet.

- *Distribution protocol* – This is the bottom-layer protocol underpinning the communication system. It allows remote clients to access STEP data in another process over the Internet. In the NIIIP project an extended version of the STEP data access interface (SDAI) was used. This interface allows data instances (e.g. individual drawing components) on a STEP database to be found, accessed and changed. Internet accessibility is achieved by binding this interface to an Internet language. CORBA was the principal mechanism used to communicate requests between SDAI compliant applications. Other languages, including Java and OLE were also used.
- *Abstraction protocol* – Many of the components used in the aircraft skin assembly incorporate thousands of different items. The practicality of IVE members managing each of these data items individually was clearly impractical. For this reason, a mechanism of bulking or abstraction was required. A language known as Express-X was used for this purpose. By abstracting the items in this way it is possible to produce more meaningful models that can be selectively imported and exported.
- *Management protocol* – The top level protocol fulfils two main roles: (1) it defines how a model can be moved between the various IVE databases, and (2) it defines how particular types of STEP data are to be navigated in relation to the various

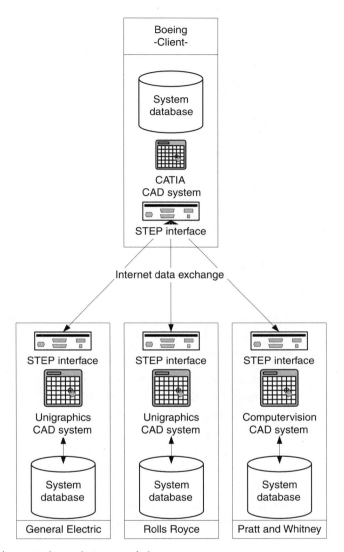

Fig. 4.3 NIIIP demonstration project system design.

abstract models. This can be compared to the role of document management systems in conventional CAD systems.

Developing functionality

The second part of the NIIIP demonstration project involved the development of specific Internet tools that could be used by the client to access and manipulate

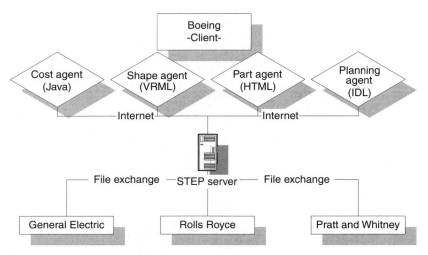

Fig. 4.4 Supported operations in the NIIIP project.

information provided by the IVEs. Another important aspect of the second part was the use of a single STEP database server, rather than a distributed set of data interfaces as shown in Figure 4.4. The client applications included:

- *Cost agent* – The purpose of the cost agent was to allow the client to estimate the assembly cost by examining the cost of its components and labour. As the agent was written as a Java applet, it enabled the client to load the client agent software at the time of execution. (An applet is a small program that can be sent along with a Web page to a user. Java applets can perform interactive immediate calculations or other simple tasks without having to send a user request back to the server.) This idea clearly has major implications for construction projects. One could envisage many subcontractors and clients, many of whom may be new to a project team, being able to access not only the data but also the necessary software at no additional cost.
- *Shape agent* – A third-party piece of software was used to visualize 3D part information, after on-line conversion of the STEP data into VRML. An alternative was to use a wire-frame viewer created as a Java applet and sent by the server.
- *Part agent* – This agent enabled two assemblies to be merged on-line in situations where they involved a common part. This was achieved using a set of options presented as HTML forms.
- *Planning agent* – Yet another Internet protocol was used for this agent. It allowed the client to interrogate a part to establish whether it formed part of an assembly.

Interoperability

The Internet promises a new way of working in architectural and engineering design. The ability to engage several design professionals simultaneously in a design process fundamentally challenges our existing model of design. No longer is it a matter of passing a single design concept through a linear process of steps, all neatly articulated in discrete domains of expertise. Instead we are faced with a more fuzzy scenario:

- An increasing number of designers become integrators. Design professionals become integration experts, with knowledge in cost estimation and building services rather than in only one of the disciplines.
- Design professionals become planning experts conscious of how the design evolution fits in a complex maze of contributors.
- Design professionals become network users able to scan resources from a global pool of information.

Replacing face-to-face interaction in design and construction

Two- and three-dimensional modelling are not the only areas with the potential to mirror services previously tied to a physical chain. Other modes of working using real-time audio and video are allowing professionals to replace the face-to-face communication process with a virtual value-adding equivalent. In an earlier chapter we considered the bias of network technology in the support of conventional thinking as opposed to intuitive thinking, sensing and emotional communication. Each of these plays an important role in almost all construction activities. Given the nature of construction projects, unfamiliar organizations must rapidly coalesce and work together with the common aim of project completion. Traditionally, face-to-face communication has played an indispensable part in this process. Questionnaire and observational studies in various industries (Sproull, 1984 and Panko, 1992) suggest that people spend between 35% and 75% of their time engaged in face-to-face interaction. There are features of face-to-face interaction that make it a preferred mode of interaction – but what are they exactly? Are all the characteristics of face-to-face interaction necessarily good? If we are proposing to use a virtual surrogate for face-to-face interaction we must have a clear understanding about how it enables us to carry out our work in the construction process.

Video conferencing is a technology that has attracted a lot of attention in the business community. This interest is often founded on the mistaken belief that it can reproduce the face-to-face experience. However, as we shall see in this chapter, there are many reasons why it falls short of being a virtual substitute.

In the construction industry the benefit of co-location explains the tendency of clients to choose local contractors, and contractors to work with local subcontractors. The physical proximity results in more frequent and informal communication that helps with collaboration. Various questionnaire studies have shown that frequent and opportunistic conversations are essential to the planning and definition phases of projects (Kraut *et al.*, 1990). Construction organizations wishing to venture into new and distant markets have to address this issue head on. The Internet solutions used by firms must be capable of replacing the face-to-face mode by communication at a distance without losing the former's essential assets. To design such a system requires not only a technological solution but also a procedural solution that complements it. Again, we see the importance of establishing a strategic understanding of construction processes before embarking on an Internet solution.

Understanding face-to-face communication

Let us reconstruct the features of face-to-face communication. Conversations involve both speakers and listeners. An obvious fact, but perhaps one less obvious fact is that these participants must co-ordinate both conversational *content* and *process* (Figure 4.5).

Co-ordination of content involves the creation of a set of shared beliefs. Moreover, these beliefs may evolve during the conversation and both speakers must share this changed circumstance – so monitoring is also required. Take for example a programming meeting ('briefing' using the European vernacular) for the design of a shopping centre. The client and contractor must come to a shared understanding of what they are seeking to build. Is it a bargain basement superstore with minimal attention to display and emphasis on efficient storage and retrieval? Is it a high-value store with emphasis on image and presentation? Is it designed to appeal to a particular income bracket or age group? The subtle understanding of cost, quality and time emphasis are more to do with a meta-level of shared values which rise above simple issues of conversation content. They are also often difficult to pinpoint in any analytical sense. This has often been one of the failings of expert systems, to capture the elusive characteristics of conversation and expertise.

Our understanding of conversation comes from much more than what is said. In practice we are able to rapidly restrict our interpretations of individual utterances because of a shared context. For example, we know that reference to 'briefs' in a construction context is unlikely to be anything to do with an article of clothing. This ability to restrict our interpretation arises in this case from a *shared linguistic*

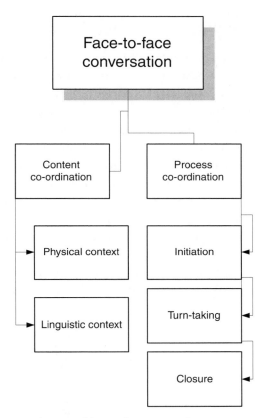

Fig. 4.5 Content and process elements of face-to-face conversation.

context. We create a vocabulary and shorthand that is particular to the construction process or a specific part of it. Another form of shared context is *physical context*. This form of shared experience arises from the fact that participants share the same set of objects and perceptual events. A contractor showing a bar chart (Gantt chart) to a client is able to make use of a physical context, and is able to guide the thought process by pointing to particular tasks. Similarly, a designer makes use of sample catalogues to show clients a range of options demonstrating their texture and mechanical properties. Another common practice is the walkthrough. This is used on construction sites and completed buildings as a highly effective form of shared physical context. It provides the cues for dialogue about site management, project progress or defect snagging, among others.

For conversation to function, only one speaker can speak at any one time. Therefore techniques are required to manage the process of speaker switching. We also need a mechanism for initiating and closing conversations. This is known as *process co-ordination*.

Nonverbal communication

The argument for introducing real-time video and video conferencing is that it enables nonverbal communication to be included in virtual conversations. This contrasts with telephony and Internet-based audio which do not provide visual feedback. In practice we know that face-to-face conversation makes use of multiple sensory inputs including voice, visual behaviour and gesture. The suggestion by some is that visual information is an indispensable requisite for co-ordinating communication content. Listener feedback in the form of head nods and eye gazes gives an indication of the listener's understanding (Kahneman, 1973). Interpersonal attitudes can be inferred from facial expressions and posture. It is also argued that nonverbal communication can help with process co-ordination. Again, head nods and eye gazes can enable speaker switching and turn-taking. If nonverbal communication is so important it discredits voice-only communication that cannot provide the necessary visual information.

These seemingly seductive arguments for video conferencing are not necessarily supported by research. Whittaker (1995) argues that technological work has

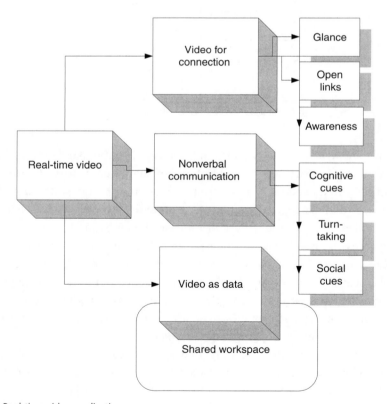

Fig. 4.6. Real-time video applications.

focused 'on one specific function of visual information, to support nonverbal communication and neglected such functions as using visual information to initiate communication or depict shared work objects.' He goes on to argue that 'previous work has overestimated the importance of supplying nonverbal information at the expense of speech.' Figure 4.6 illustrates the application areas of real-time video.

Technical trade-offs

Video conferencing still has to overcome substantial technical barriers. The high data rates required by video mean that compression has to be used. This necessitates the use of compression and decompression techniques that produce transmission lags. Added to this are the network delays over the Internet itself. The result is a time-delayed transmission that greatly impedes interpersonal communication. Because of this, it is common for a video-based conference to be less effective than audio only, as audio-only transmissions are not hampered by the additional overhead of video compression. Furthermore, sound quality can be further upgraded to make use of additional bandwidth. At this point we begin to see the importance of understanding face-to-face communication and how synchronization and bandwidth allocation of Internet systems become critical design issues. Inevitably we are faced with trade-off issues.

Cognitive cueing

We have already mentioned how listener's cues such as head nods and facial expressions provide the speaker with clues about the listener's understanding and attention. Chapanis *et al.* (1972) examined this phenomenon and compared the effectiveness of a variety of task outcome measures, such as time to solve a problem and quality of solution. In one of these tasks, individuals had to collaborate in constructing a mechanical object. One person had the physical component and the other had the instructions. The research was conducted using two types of media input – audio-only communication and high quality video/audio. The studies showed that adding visual information did not increase the speed of problem solving or the quality of the solution. Other research supports this finding, indicating that speech is the critical medium to enable collaborative problem solving. Whittaker (1995) cites a number of other laboratory studies showing the minimal contribution of visual information to cognitive problem solving (Short *et al.*, 1976; Reid, 1977). What is even more surprising is that this does not only relate to video quality: even face-to-face interaction performs no better than speech-only communication in such tasks.

Turn-taking

Would visual information help with the orderly progress of Internet-based discussions in construction site meetings or design meetings? Objective and subjective studies on turn-taking (process co-ordination) present slightly conflicting results. These studies have looked at how video can help in supporting interactivity, selective attention and the ability of speakers to initiate conversation. In objective studies (Whittaker and O'Conaill, 1993) key measures such as pausing, overlapping speech and interruption management were examined. What was evident from these studies is that individuals adopt a formal method for handing over conversation (such as identifying the next speaker) using video conferencing as opposed to face-to-face conversation. This significantly added to the overhead of process co-ordination. The limitation of video conferencing was attributed to the absence of directional sound or visual cues such as head turning that are absent when presented on flat VDU monitors. Subjective studies presented more positive feedback on the value of video. Video/audio was perceived as providing more interactivity, allowing individuals to listen selectively to speakers, and for speakers to monitor listeners' attention.

Social cueing

Many of the interactions in construction involve conflict resolution, bargaining and negotiation. Access to visual information allows participants to focus more on the motives of others. It can be argued that conversations are more personalized, less argumentative and produce outcomes that are different in nature to communication not supported by video. One important finding was that meetings are less likely to end in deadlock compared to speech-only meetings. The studies by Short *et al.* (1976) also suggest that people tend to end up liking each other more – a laudable situation for construction meetings!

Internet-based real-time video

The Internet generally supports only low-quality video. NetMeeting, produced by Microsoft, is a low-cost system that has attracted much interest in this area. Its ability to support multiple windows means that several locations can be seen simultaneously.

Studies of low-quality video systems indicate that, in certain circumstances, adding visual information can detract from the interaction processes, if video is allowed to interfere with the audio element. This can occur in two ways: (a) by the transmission delay caused by compression and decompression, and (b) by the enforcement of half-duplexing that allows only unidirectional transmission of audio at any one point in time.

Video-as-data

The work of Whittaker (1995) and others suggests that too much attention has been given to nonvisual communication. Perhaps the greatest potential for video technology in construction communication is when it is used in combination with other Internet applications enabling the creation of shared workspaces (Tang & Rua, 1994). It can be used to provide information about the remote participant's attentional focus. This leads to the concept of what Gaver *et al.* (1992) term 'video-as-data'. In their experiments participants were able to choose between various views of an object under study as well as images of other participants. They found that people consistently chose images of an object (49% of the time) in preference to facial views of their co-participant. This reinforces the argument that information on the shared physical context is more important that information about gaze and gesture of the participants for design processes.

Video for connection

A common problem with electronic communication technologies is that, unlike face-to-face communication, they do not lend themselves to opportunistic interactions. When we encounter people in the work setting we are easily able to assess their availability – we can see whether they are involved in a task or dealing with another person. Technologies such as the telephone are often seen as intrusive, as they take no account of the user's availability. Hence the need to use secretaries as gatekeepers and the ever increasing voice-mail chase that undermines the value of telephone as a communication medium. Experiments with video have been used to provide visual information to facilitate connection for unplanned interactions. These 'video for connection' technologies fall into one of three types:

- *Glance* – This allows users to briefly 'drop in' on a colleague to assess their availability.
- *Open links* – These provide persistent video and audio channels between two locations.
- *Awareness* – Applications that involve the use of periodic sampling to provide an update of someone's availability (notice that this differs from glance in that the information is asynchronous – i.e. a single frame updated periodically).

Experiments with open links have been conducted by Bellcore and Xerox PARC to link geographically separated sites. These experiments showed that 70% of open link usage were related to opportunistic drop-ins. However, most of these interactions were brief in nature and were not seen as effective in supporting work (Fish *et al.*, 1993). Perhaps of more interest to Internet applications are awareness and glance facilities, which require much less Internet traffic. Glance systems are reported as showing very high failure rates, with 97% being terminated without conversation. However, this might be seen as a positive characteristic as the system is serving the purpose of communicating availability. The failure rate is more a measure of how often people were not available – and as such is not a reflection of how effective the system is. Many of the failures occurred because people were out of their room.

Reality of mirroring the face-to-face experience

In summary we can see how trying to reproduce the face-to-face interaction using the Internet, although possible in principle, is fraught with difficulties. The overriding difficulty is the limitation of bandwidth that severely curtails system performance. This limitation suggests that we should accept trade-offs between visual and auditory communication and channel our efforts to the medium that is most effective. Future developments in fibre optics and high-speed networks will undoubtedly improve the prospects of using real-time applications but for the moment we should treat much of the hype with scepticism. Perhaps one of the most dramatic applications of real-time video over the Internet is the ability to transmit site information to the design office. Clever workarounds to reduce bandwidth demands including compression and time-lapsed imaging may overcome the performance difficulties mentioned so far.

Taywood Engineering

Who is using innovative Internet technology to mirror the physical value chain in construction? The following case study describes a project undertaken by Taylor Woodrow and highlights the possibilities for mirroring capabilities in construction. It demonstrates how the Internet can be used not just to make information more visible – but to create a wholly new business activity. Taywood Engineering are the engineering arm of Taylor Woodrow that has its main headquarters in London, UK, but operates globally, from Southern California to Kuala Lumpur and Ghana. It has a very succinct mission statement: 'Invent the future: manage the change', and this is reflected in their Internet strategy.

One section of Taywood Engineering, the modelling group, is looking to provide a visualization and knowledge-based engineering solution for clients. They have recently engaged in work with a progressive client that is seeking to construct 24 unmanned power stations distributed throughout the UK. The client recognizes the opportunities of a niche market in providing peak demand electricity for industrial on-site customers and local housing, using open-cycle stations and combined heat and power solutions. These stations are small gas-fired stations providing 50 MW of power. At the outset Taywood Engineering wanted to promote the idea of an integrated project team for the programme which would involve the construction of up to 15 power stations at any one time. The power stations would be based on three or four different blueprints and the learning curve when progressing from one station to the next would be significant provided a mechanism was put into place to allow this information to be shared between jobs.

Taywood proposed an Internet solution to the information issue as part of a bid for the project. The novel information management solution was central to Taywood winning the contract. Project information, including documentation, site progress photographs and CAD drawings, is maintained by an information manager. These are available at increasing levels of detail for use from top-down within the client organization. The managing director can obtain summary executive information, the contracts manager can elicit more detailed information, and the project management teams with one project manager on each site have very specific information about the progress of all of the 24 sites. The Internet system is also a key project management tool for Taywood for carrying out the project.

The system is driven by Web-enabled databases that serve up different tiers of information for each of the different users. Standard database software, Access^{TM}, is used to store the data, and middleware software (Cold Fusion^{TM}) provides the necessary link to produce Web pages visible to the client. Using this system, users are able to update information on site and find out about progress on other sites.

For numerical data such as cost data, Microsoft^{TM} Excel files are used in conjunction with a Web browser, which opens up the application automatically (is spawned) when spreadsheet information is requested. Cost plans and cost monitoring information such as outturn costs and percentage of work complete are available for the quantity surveyors.

Document management is an important part of the system. Documents include static documents, which remain fixed throughout the project, and dynamic documents, which are likely to be changed or created during the course of the project. Static documents available to people involved in the project include health and safety, specification documents, method statements, quality plans and tender submissions.

Drawings including general arrangement drawings are stored on a central server as AutoCAD^{TM} files. One particular file format (DWF) is used for read-only applications. The benefit of this file format is that it has been designed specifically for Internet transmission, by making use of high compression methods which produce very compact files (often as small as 15% of the original AutoCAD drawing). A plug-in, which like many others is available for downloading free of charge on the Internet, is used by the client to view these drawings. The plug-in, known as Whip^{TM}, has many of the functional characteristics of a complete drawing package, allowing the user to view various layers of a drawing, to zoom in on specific details and to hotlink to related information by clicking on a particular part of the drawing (this requires that an Internet link has been embedded in the original AutoCAD drawing). The client is thus able to scrutinize drawings without having to go to the expense of purchasing dedicated software.

Photographic information obtained at regular intervals from each of the power station sites is made available on the Web system. This enables a quick progress comparison with other sites. For sites yet to get underway, the records provide an invaluable source of detail information. Only some of the power stations in the programme of work will have received planning permission at the point when construction begins on the first few. The cost of a planning enquiry for any of the proposed sites would be financially prohibitive, so any measures which can help to establish a rapport with local planning authorities or local lobbies are likely to help with increasing the speed of programme completion. For this reason, the Web system could be designed to cater for the information needs of planners and local interest groups. Using this approach, planners can look at the impact of a similar power station project, both in relation to the construction phase and upon completion. Local inhabitants could log on from their computer at home or from a local library and obtain information about the likely impact of the power station, including the benefits to the local community.

The value of the Internet in this solution is its ability to bring together many different forms of information (including database records, photographs and documents) and present them within a single Web browser environment.

Taywood clearly obtain a number of benefits as project managers and designers in the programme:

- A clearer understanding with the client minimizing the likelihood of design changes.
- A significant reduction in paper production in the form of drawings and reports.
- An opportunity to maximize the learning curve from one project to the next.
- An opportunity to become involved in a partnering arrangement through the use of a shared technology and information system.
- An increased likelihood of follow-on work during the operational phase due to their familiarity with the system.

From the other side of the win-win equation the client stands to gain from:

- The cost and efficiency saving arising from the rapid learning cycle, enabled by Internet information exchange.
- Risk reduction through access to up-to-date site information and cost monitoring data.
- The ability to provide certain information to a much larger public audience and to establish a dialogue with potential opponents to placate their concerns about the development.

What happens at the end of the programme? The fact that information has been stored in a homogeneous and accessible form means that life-time records can be readily added during the operational phase. As the power stations are unmanned, remote monitoring forms an important part of this phase. Telemetry is one technology that has proven to work very effectively over the Internet. Telemetry is the science of continuously recording the condition of a system using electronic signals. Traditionally this has been undertaken locally or by downloading information in batch mode. Using the Internet it is possible to visually track many types of condition data with scrolling graphs which appear on the Web browser. This kind of technology is indicative of the way that construction programmes will continue to go. The information systems used during construction will increasingly become enmeshed with the operational phase. Construction firms that are sufficiently entrepreneurial will seize this opportunity to have a greater contribution to make in the value chain and also obtain a greater understanding of how their buildings perform after completion.

KEY POINTS FROM THIS CHAPTER

- Internet-enabled CAD and object modelling offer significant opportunities for co-design over the Internet.

- These technologies will also enable many stakeholders to visualize and understand design proposals as they emerge.

- The advent of Internet-enabled design will demand a change in the design process and will involve new professionals and new services.

- Other new services that replace face-to-face communication will prevail, but trade-offs need to be made to ensure a rich experience.

- Construction firms are already beginning to realize opportunities for new services and new ways of adding value with Internet technology.

5

Creating customer communities

Questions addressed in this chapter

- Is there an alternative to electronic knowledge bases as a way of getting closer to customers and suppliers?

- Can the Internet be used to enrich human-to-human interaction in the construction process?

- What types of construction firm are likely to benefit from a more direct on-line interaction?

- What are the limitations of conference technologies currently in use and what are they likely to be superseded by?

- What is the future of on-line communities in construction and how will this affect the day-to-day activities of construction firms?

We believe that communications have to do something nontrivial with the information they send and receive. And ... to interact with the richness of living information – not merely in the passive way that we have become accustomed to using books and libraries, but as active participants in an ongoing process, bringing something to it through our interaction with it, and not simply receiving from it by our connection to it. (Licklider and Taylor, 1968; founders of the Internet).

Introduction

The exploitation of Internet technology should go further than creating value for the construction firm. A firm should be able to *extract* value from it. Having developed a parallel value chain, firms are able to exploit the Internet to build customer relationships. The information is used not just to enable firms to undertake their work, but also as a value-added element for the client.

We have looked at the way in which Internet technology can make construction project information more visible. But doing things more efficiently is not the only way in which the Internet can help us. Indeed, if we constrain our attention to operational efficiencies we are missing the key capability of the Internet – its capacity to reinforce learning relationships between customers, clients and producers. The construction industry is a business of mass customization and one-to-one marketing. This chapter looks at the possibilities for assimilating attitudes and beliefs that form such an important part of this process and the possibilities provided by on-line communities.

The Internet was conceived with the notion of 'community' in mind. Licklider and Taylor (1968) described their vision as an 'intergalactic computer network' and defined four principles for the computer:

- Communication is defined as an interactive creative process.
- Response times need to be short to make the 'conversation' free and easy.
- Larger networks form out of smaller regional networks.
- Communities form out of affinity and common interests.

However, this idea of community is not just based on philanthropic thinking. Trading communities are becoming a vital linchpin for construction firms. Designer, planners and builders are also becoming aware of the increasingly complex nature of clients with whom they deal. These stakeholders are no longer represented by a single individual but by a whole community of people, who are evolving and interacting over time. Understanding the dynamics of these communities and becoming a part of them is becoming the key to business success.

Hans Haenlein Architects

At this point the concept of community might seem a bit vague. In order to highlight just how strategic an understanding of a community can be, we will look at one firm – Hans Haenlein Architects. It is not remarkable in terms of using the Internet. Indeed it reflects the current position of many firms in the construction industry that are still positioning themselves in relation to this technology. What the case study does reveal is just how sophisticated the 'community' nature of briefing and design is and how it relies on rich 'face-to-face' communication with stakeholders. After looking at this case study we will examine whether the Internet has anything to offer firms like this – firms that have invested heavily in the personalization of information that is carefully engineered to reflect the needs of the client. This information is not easily codified and is tacit in nature.

We will also see how many of the assumptions about the use of the Internet are based on incorrect views about the motivations and aspirations of firms. This case study brings the issue of electronic commerce over the Internet closer to home. It illustrates that many firms involved in the construction process are small to medium sized. Moreover, they may not simply be seeking to maximize profits. Professional practices are trying to develop a greater rapport with potential and actual clients. This relationship inevitably involves not just one individual, but rather a whole community of individuals and committees. Furthermore, although the membership of this community may change, its existence may live on long after the completion of a single facility. Given this very different agenda we can see how the Internet promises a reconciliation between the purchaser and the provider of a service.

Hans Haenlein Architects was established by Hans Haenlein in a converted terrace town house in Hammersmith, London, back in 1963. Since then its size has fluctuated to reach an acceptable maximum of between seven and nine employees – the size being constrained by the physical capacity of the building itself. The practice is rarely short of work and has never felt the need to externalize its activities. Hans Haenlein describe themselves as 'misfits' with respect to the absence of any form of self-advertisement. Rarely do they publish about buildings they have been involved with. 'Nothing beyond the word of mouth' is the phrase used. The practice's size is typical of many small businesses in the UK. Firms with no more than nine people represent 90% of all UK businesses and account for 50% of the private sector workforce. The architectural firm operates in a UK construction industry that is craft dominated. Compared with international competition, this industry typically has low input costs, low profit margins but high output costs.

To understand a potential Internet strategy for such a firm we need to understand the complex characteristics of the service it provides. The practice has developed expertise and experience in educational facilities. It has focused its attention on the procurement side and in particular the front end or briefing (programming) element. Like many modern businesses customer focus increasingly means having an in-depth understanding of the customer's business. Hans Haenlein Architects have taken this to an extreme – they actively advise on curriculum analysis. This involves considerations of educational activities, timetabling and resourcing. Having a knowledge of the curriculum issues allows the architectural firm to talk knowledgeably about whether a client actually needs a new facility! The current briefing (programming) process in the UK simply involves a *statement of need*. This presupposes that a client involved in the brief actually understands their need. Hans Haenlein Architects have tried to open up the scope of the brief to include more than the statement of need. Three other aspects are considered in the brief:

- The business of the client – Where is it at? Where is it going? At what pace?
- The real-estate position of the client – this may involve further analysis and information from energy surveys or post-occupancy studies.
- The communication characteristics of the client organization – Who is accountable to whom? How are decisions reached? How are cultural norms established?

One of the innovations of the practice introduced in 1981 is that of fee-based construction management for the procurement of educational buildings. The practice became increasingly conscious of the obstructive nature of conventional procurement methods involving general contracting (typically under a Joint Contracts Tribunal (JCT)-type contract often used in the UK). Invariably this approach distanced the designer from the 'people at the coal face', as Hans expresses it. By this he is referring to the trade and specialist contractors. By removing the middle man they believe that they can achieve a better product, at a lower cost and in a more timely manner. Using the construction management approach, one key trade contractor, typically the builder, would take responsibility for site safety, security and lighting. Other trades such as brickwork, plastering and painting would cooperate with the building contractor and all would be direct signatories to a contract with the client. As the construction management firm, Hans Haenlein Architects are then able to focus on running the project.

Often clients will ask for a quick sketch early on. The practice try to avoid such early framing processes – preferring instead to focus the client's mind on a more creative solution. Establishing the client's preference for a capital-intensive or a revenue-intensive solution is an important element in this – specifically when developing an appropriate life-cycle cost model.

With educational buildings, the practice are invariably dealing with multiple clients. Representatives from the Board of Governors, the Diocese, the local education authority and members of staff from the school are all likely to be involved. To deal with such a situation, the various stakeholders are encouraged to buy into a strong management process. This requires a commitment on the part of each of the client representatives. The practice take the unusual step of applying their own selection test:

> to observe ... the different client groups ... how they take 'possession' of the building. Unless they embrace it ... are proud of it ... it will fail.

To engender a sense of ownership and improve communication, a development steering committee is set up. This committee will meet up regularly throughout the design and construction phases. Hans Haenlein encourages the group to think in a 'designerly' way – an informal way that is empathetic to the design process.

The IT arrangement in the practice is typical of many in UK architectural offices. A local server-based network operates in the building. The CAD program Minicad^{TM}

is used as the main draughting tool. One part of their IT which they have invested heavily in (in terms of man-hours) is the computerization of the job process. The computer system that they have developed, known as COMPASS, is modelled on the RIBA (Royal Institute of British Architects) *Job Book*. This formalized method provides a framework for coordinating the running of a job. It deals with the issuing of instructions and forms to contractors. The practice developed COMPASS to streamline the internal job management system and it now provides an invaluable part of their administrative set-up.

So how does the Internet fit within the practice's plans? Haenlein acknowledges the need to give themselves a public face: 'The Internet provides a marvelous opportunity to make ourselves more transparent'. He acknowledges that a lot of visitors to their website are likely to turn away with no follow-through – the hope is that those who do respond will be the right ones. Only by providing a fairly complex set of messages can this be achieved and the Internet provides an ideal medium for this. One of the developments that prompted the practice to develop its own website was the advent of the RIBA's website. This site provides a complete directory of RIBA registered practices in the UK covering several thousand companies. As such it provides a key point of reference for clients seeking suitable architects. It was seen as useful to provide a link to a much more detailed and maintainable Web site for Hans Haenlein Architects through this central reservoir.

As to the possibility of using the Internet for integrated project management, the practice is constrained by the technologies currently being used by consultants and clients. In 2 years' time they believe that this situation is likely to be significantly different. The ability to use integrated project information using standards such as the layering standard advocated by Autodesk will further stimulate networked systems.

From this case study there are a number of observations that can be made as an outsider:

- Our assumptions about the motives for construction firms to engage in e-commerce are not always self-evident. Attracting more clients or more business may not be the primary objective. The purpose of e-commerce may be to achieve a better matching process between client and architect. Clients choose architects as a result of a more informed selection process. The Internet provides opportunities for a single point of reference for such comparative information as exemplified by the RIBA *Directory of Practices*. For Hans Haenlein Architects the interest is in acquiring clients who understand why they have chosen them in preference to competitors. In doing so, the process of managing a project is likely to be smoother and the final product more in line with their needs.
- Messages are complex. How a company communicates its message is not akin to 'offloading boxes from a lorry'. It is more like fishing for a very elusive fish.

Practices such as Hans Haenlein Architects possess a wealth of company knowledge. This extends to process innovations, which in this case study can be seen in the use of information technology to document and manage jobs. The Internet allows such systems to be externalized very quickly. This might take the form of simple on-line provision of database information to colleagues in the practice located at remote sites. Going beyond this, it could be used as a value-added element allowing clients to eavesdrop on project progress.

Observing the characteristics of the architectural practice you can quickly see possibilities that could be explored in terms of the ability to manage other architectural firms' jobs using the system already in use by the practice. This moves into another stage in the virtual value chain where firms are able to create income from a completely new source by mirroring capabilities. As such, the firm could provide a data warehousing capability – the value-added element being the copyright of the job management process in electronic form. Firms may not see this as desirable if it allows competitors to quickly mimic their own business processes; however, if the other party is not likely to be competing in the same geographical area or client sector, selling on the business process model as an interactive Web-based system may provide a significant source of income.

The case study highlights how a seemingly small firm can develop highly sophisticated learning relationships. It shows in particular a clear production/delivery strategy, with the use of sophisticated briefing tools to enable the client to express their building needs. It also illustrates the formation of an assessment strategy, whereby clients are assessed in terms of their life-time worth to the design practice. The dialogue and insights provided by clients enable the practice to extend their capabilities in the educational sector and apply it to other sectors

Power of the on-line community

What does the technology of today offer for firms seeking to be involved in communities in the virtual world as well as the physical world? Construction websites rarely encourage communication among visitors. But customers themselves are beginning to get together on-line to pool their expertise and share views about manufacturers, contractors and consultants. One of the main tools being used to enable on-line interaction are electronic discussion groups. These can be set up by host sites with minimal investment and can take one of three forms:

- *List servers* – These servers handle subscription requests from email users who are added to a discussion group. Subsequent email postings by individual members are then sent to everyone on the list. To prevent a proliferation of emails, sent messages are often assembled as a single archived message.

- *Newsgroup/Usenet* – A newsgroup is a globally accessible network of interest groups provided through the Usenet service. Usenet makes use of a specific protocol on the Internet known as network news transfer protocol (NNTP). The system presents subjects in a hierarchical manner. Newsgroup members can view postings and see message threads on line. Postings can be made in response to other people's comments and these are appended to the discussion thread. Most Web browsers can communicate using the NNTP protocol.
- *Web conference boards* – Web conference boards provide all the functionality of newsgroups, but retain messages on the host side rather than on the user's local computer. The World Wide Web is increasingly being used in preference to list servers and newsgroups. Such systems bypass the need to register a formal news-group service. Moreover, those organizations hosting a Web-based conference are able to moderate the site and analyse the usage statistics. The archiving process enables users to search the postings to see whether particular issues have been discussed recently.

Examples of on-line discussions

To help in explaining the qualities of on-line discussion in construction, the following section presents three discussion threads, each with a particular flavour. All of the dis-cussions appear on the AECinform Website (www.aecinform.com). Construction-related discussion forums can be found on a number of websites on the Internet. Although some postings on these forums are trivial in content, other professionals regularly volunteer ideas and information on standard practices around the world.

Re: Quantity Surveys

Thread on the Construction Law discussion forum of the AECinform Website

The 'quantity survey' discussion involves some interesting banter across the Atlantic, starting with a US architect wishing that quantity surveys formed part of the American bidding process. An exchange then ensues between a US- and UK-based practitioner, followed by a US practitioner who explains the system used in Utah.

Posted by Bryan on January 25, 1998 at 07:23:13 PM EST:

The United States is one of the only countries in the world that does not include quantity surveys with the bidding documents (quantity survey lists amounts of all materials to build something, the bidder fills in the unit costs). This does increase the architect's liability but should make negotiating a change order much easier and limits the opportunity for a contractor to say it is not in my bid. Does anyone have any comments about implementation of this type of system in the American market?

Posted by Sam Finney on April 27, 1998 at 09:52:25 PM EDT:

I would very much like to talk with you about quantity survey practice in Europe. I too wonder why Americans do not provide this service, and am attempting to figure out how to provide it. I read your thread of January, and point out that while most architects or owners on larger projects do get estimates, the fact is that the estimate is not very good. Anyway, if you care to respond, I would be interested in hearing what you know about the practice, and I could tell you some of my ideas for creating quantity estimates for use by contractors, designers, and owners alike. (Why is every party along the way to construction paying to do their own surveys, and why is the owner paying to have it done by the general contractor, and the designer too?!)

Posted by Richard Allen on January 26, 1998 at 08:10:40 PM EST:

I disagree. The US market especially on public works projects usually uses unit price bids with quantities. When the quantities differ, the project generally closes out with a balancing change order. If the quantities differ greatly, the contractor is entitled to a price variation.

Posted by Ron Snowden on February 09, 1998 at 09:41:28 PM EST:

In Utah the general practice for Architects designing public (state) projects is to provide estimates of cost to the state as part of their contract responsibility. Typically, 3 estimates are provided – schematic design (SD), design development (DD) and construction documents (CD). An architect is foolish to proceed with his design without ongoing estimates because if the project exceeds the budget the firm will be responsible for redesign to the budget. Architects are usually not in touch with costs well enough to perform accurate estimates. A professional estimator is usually well worth what they charge – as many dollars are at risk with a contract tied to a specific budget.

Re: Design Build – a can of worms?

Posted to the Design Build discussion forum of the AECinform Website

The 'can of worms' discussion is prompted by an engineer who puts forward his misgivings about Design Build from a quality point of view. The first respondent to the message appears to be a moderator of the group. He presents a similarly sceptical view of the Design Build procurement method. The final respondent is forthright in defending Design Build and questions the competence of the two previous writers to make judgements about the method. The reader is conscious of the diversity of geographical and sectoral splits probably represented by the different writers. The discussion provides emotional, technical and professional revelations!

Posted by Barry J Hunt on December 15, 1997 at 07:24:50 AM EST:

I spent much time investigating damage from bomb blasts at a number of buildings in London, England. Most of the recently built structures were Design Build and some interesting things were found when we determined their condition. Rather than go into all the details I will highlight one of our major findings. The external envelope was at most risk from a blast and we assessed a wide range of stone cladding systems using dye testing and other techniques. We found that much of the damage that resulted from the blast was already present and needed little to help tip it over the precipice of failure – in some instances stones were not even bolted to the building! Some of the stone was obviously in such a poor condition when it went on to the building we wondered how it had the gall to have stayed up – insurers of public indemnity should take a sharp intake of breath. We believed that had the building practices common before Design Build been implemented and the cladding ensured that it was of a reasonable standard, then probably over 90% if not all of the cladding would not have failed. We have determined natural stones in the quarry and the stone yard have cracks not visible to the naked eye and some of these are potentially disastrous for cladding situations, but still no one is checking. This has been just one small but worrying example of Design Build, there must be more sophisticated independent checking.

Posted by Al on December 20, 1997 at 02:26:48 PM EST:

Barry,
Good point, it sounds like a case of the fox watching the chicken coop. Even though problems arise from the "old" style of building, mistakes or shortcuts are more often caught because there are individual entities involved. I can see "a few good points" of Design Build but they're outweighed by the possibilities of errors such as you have talked about. I'm NOT an advocate of Design Build from what I've seen and heard. Money is the bottom line and its hard enough to be a professional in one trade let alone getting involved with everyone else's business. Like I've stated in past posts, it seems like the only one that benefits from this is the designer. He can do a little less research on items and be assured that everyone

else will correct them. Advocates of Design Build, I'm going to start another thread with a scenario for you to give me your input in case I'm still not seeing this in the right perspective, hope to see some discussion from everyone on it.

Posted by Joseph Yencho on August 24, 1998 at 22:13:01:

Sorry guys, major disagreement here. As a Design Builder for 15 years, I have found that the customer gets MORE for their money than LESS. The object of the Design Builder is to give the customer as much as they can reasonably AFFORD. They set the budget. I show them what I can design and build for them at that price. Price overruns will not occur if both parties are in agreement from the beginning. AND if the DB is competent I will grant you not every DB is actually capable in this area BUT this goes for EVERYONE else in the industry equally. If I had a dollar for every pie in the sky – completely infeasible – project handed to me for bid from ARCHITECTS ... I wouldn't be here. ... I'd be retired in the Caribbean. As for the previous comment "I've been involved" – I would like to know YOUR CREDENTIALS ... and why you're constantly involved in bad projects?

Re: Real user discussion of project management package

Thread on the Software/Management discussion forum of the AECinform Website

One part of the design/construction community that is particularly proactive in using Web-based forums is the IT community, using project management software or design software. Web forums provide an ideal mechanism for software vendors to stimulate discussion and elicit feedback about their products. Ideas are generated about innovative ways of using a technology and unanticipated applications. These discussion forums inevitably have an ebb and flow of activity associated with the hotness of the topic or the product. Users will often produce solutions to problems that even the manufacturers had not worked out. The following thread starts off with a writer appealing for unbiased opinions about available project management software. As always, the software vendor cannot resist posting a sales pitch, but the author eventually receives a response from someone at a similar position in the decision-making process.

Posted by Susan Ferguson on May 21, 1998 at 02:24:17 PM EDT:

I am looking to discuss project management systems with actual users of such systems (i.e. Prolog Manager, Expedition, etc...). I am interested in finding out what the real benefits have been to users – not what the salesperson says will be the benefits. I am trying to figure out if different packages benefit different kinds of company environments. I would also be interested in talking to another Design Build firm about this topic.

Posted by Brien Harvey on June 25, 1998 at 16:28:53:

If you would like a list of design/build references who are successfully using Prolog Manager, let me know and I will e-mail you a list.

Posted by Jason Galts on July 05, 1998 at 18:54:13:

I work as a Construction Manager for a Design Build firm and I have just recently acquired Prolog Manager from MPS. However, I have not used it long enough to give you an accurate picture. Based on my requirements it appears to be the right solution but time will tell. It is weak on faxing and communicating compared to Expedition but it integrates much better with MS Office and Project 98. MPS tells me that these problems will be resolved in 4–6 months.

All of the discussions above challenge our existing understanding of e-commerce. E-commerce is no longer about vendors setting-up stall for consumers to view their wares. Consumers and clients are now able to take a more proactive approach (with or without facilitation from vendors). The ability to identify other clients with similar requirements from a much larger pool of individuals (global) greatly accelerates their learning process. Their trust in the opinion of other consumers is likely to be much greater than in that of the product and service providers. The challenge for product and service providers in the construction industry is to ensure that they monitor and respond to ideas and opinions generated in these on-line communities.

The future of on-line communities

The electronic discussion mechanisms for on-line communities do have limitations. The previous examples of discussion threads show some of these. Although members of a discussion group may share a common interest, their objectives may vary widely. Some may be trying to elicit second opinions; others may be looking for solutions; some may be trying to sell their services; and others may simply be looking to establish camaraderie. It should be said that in some respects, electronic discussions have advantages over a real-life community. Because they rely on text entry, information can be stored indefinitely, allowing others to pick up on a threaded discussion whenever they encounter it. In this way, themes have the potential to grow in an organic way. But the slow take-up by users reflects some of the limitations of this technology. Hattori *et al.* (1999) point out three of these problems:

- How to bring people together. The use of search engines and on-line directories can help in this process, but a more effective method is required. How does a client considering a new type of air-conditioning system identify other users currently making use of such a system?
- How to enable smooth communication. One of the problems for the user is understanding the context of discussion groups. How do themes relate and in what direction are they developing? Systems are needed for visualizing and sharing common contexts.
- How to establish the relationship between people. Affinities between people are multidimensional. It is not just a question of having a common interest in lighting design or quantity surveying. Objectives may differ, the desired level of intimacy may vary, industry sector and geographic location may be very different.
- People's interests are unique and dynamic, changing over time. Individuals need a visual representation of communities that are specific to their own perspective.

Socialware

Socialware is a term coined by Hattori *et al.* (1999) to describe a decentralized system designed to encourage opportune meetings and discussions on the Internet. It represents a radical advance away from the centralized model currently used. It differs from groupware, that is only appropriate for people already organized to work co-operatively. Socialware is designed to be adaptive and and reflect changing issues over time.

One example of socialware is the CommunityOrganizer developed by Hattori *et al.* (1999). It revolves around the use of agents. On the Internet, an agent (also known as an intelligent agent) is a small program that gathers information or performs some other service without your immediate presence and on some regular schedule. Typically, an agent program, using parameters you have provided, searches all or some part of the Internet, gathers information you are interested in, and presents it to you on a daily or other periodic basis. These agents are typically mobile and are able to act remotely on your behalf. The CommunityOrganizer system is designed around two systems:

- *Personal units* – Such units are made up of the user, supported by a group of personal agents. A personal agent may be domain specific (for example heating, ventilation and air-conditioning (HVAC), formwork or CAD software) or more generic (for example, an interface agent for navigating and reading documents).

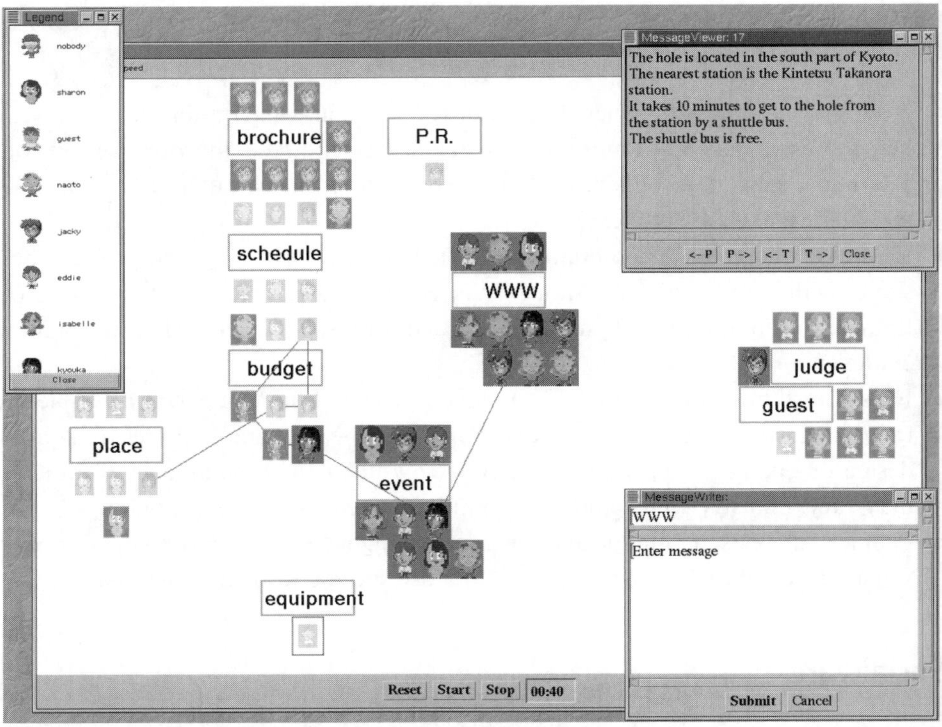

Fig. 5.1 Visualization of discussion groups using CommunityOrganizer.

- *Community agents* – These agents provide shared information, knowledge or contexts within the community, acting as mediators between people. They are able to collect user profiles and identify potential communities.

In order to visualize communities via the Web, the system personal agents are used to display the structure of discussions according to the user's interests. In the integrated viewspace, messages are shown as icons. The person, topic and importance are represented by the type, position and shading of the icon. For example, icons for messages become dimmer and smaller as the importance decreases. The importance is calculated as a function of time, reputation and interest for the topics of messages, as shown in Figure 5.1.

The relevance between users is calculated by the community agent with reference to the user's profiles. These in turn can be obtained from each user's input, either directly or from other user inputs such as searches of mailing list archives, or searches of personal web pages. Personal agents provide on-screen slidebars that allow the user to adjust the weightings of viewpoints. These include such things as location, type, content and intimacy. The slidebar preference system is shown in Figure 5.2.

All of the agents are written in Java so any on-line user is able to interact with the agents using a standard Web browser. Innovations such as CommunityOrganizer

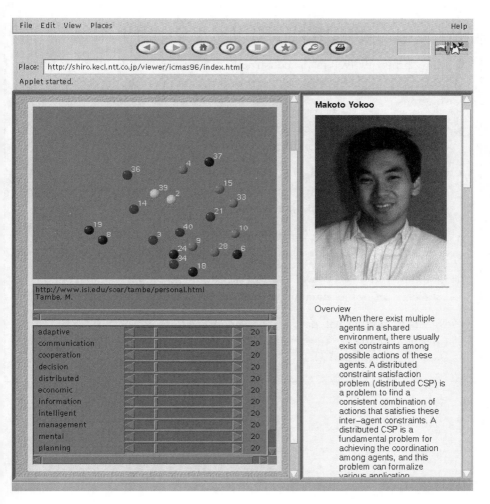

Fig. 5.2 Defining user profiles using CommunityOrganizer.

promise to transform the utility of on-line communities. However, there are many communities that are already active in the construction sector, based on proven and simple technologies such as list servers. It may be difficult to get such groups to migrate over to such radically different agent-based systems. What is clear from all of this is the commercial possibilities of informal on-line communication. Whether you are a specifier choosing a building product, a client identifying potential partners, or a manufacturer promoting a product, the possibilities for using these informal mechanisms are immense. However, it will require a change in mindset regarding our attitudes to openness and creative activities in the workplace.

KEY POINTS FROM THIS CHAPTER

- Many firms involved in the construction process, particularly the design profession, require a very rich person-to-person interaction to achieve solutions.

- On-line communities, because of their openness, will enable firms to capture more information from employees, clients and suppliers.

- Existing on-line conferencing technologies are difficult for users to understand. Conventional threaded discussions may be impersonal and the subject matter may be of limited relevance.

- Emerging technologies will enable users to visualize other community members in a much more graphic and multifaceted way.

- Emerging technologies will enable users to identify affinities and common problems with other community members in a much more visual way.

- New communities will develop in the construction industry as a result of Internet technology. In particular, clients and customers will begin to share know-how and experiences of products and services.

6

Creating trust

Questions addressed in this chapter

- What is the significance of trust in the construction industry?

- Does the Internet have implications for trust in the construction industry?

- How do we entrust information to project partners?

- What types of Internet activity are likely to compromise trust and security?

- What types of security measures should be sought to combat intellectual theft between organizations involved in a project and from outsiders?

- Should a new 'trust model' be adopted by construction firms in the age of the Internet?

Introduction

Trust is the name of the game. In an earlier chapter we saw how the economics of information is being redefined by new rules. For good reason, many construction firms are uneasy about the new rules. Electronic commerce over the Internet does indeed improve the interchange of information between trading partners. But in so doing, it increases the risks of opportunistic behaviour by collaborators. Construction firms become more vulnerable by revealing not just data but process information. They reveal systems and methods for managing projects that have evolved and been refined over many years. The transparency of these systems, when implemented in a networked environment, make them easily transferable. Although this open environment can prove to be very useful as a means of assimilating new project partners into your preferred way of working, it also raises the possibility of losing intellectual capital by a process of diffusion or opportunistic exploitation. Trust constitutes a cornerstone of new interorganizational relationships developing in the construction industry. In this chapter we will see that Internet technologies can provide secure trading environments, but firms must learn to develop what Ratnasingham (1998) calls 'complete trustworthy relationships'.

Transaction costs and opportunism

Why do we see more talk of collaboration in building procurement? Long-term cooperation between firms, strategic alliances, joint ventures, partnering, licensing and networks are the hot topics in the construction press. The complex web of interorganizational behaviour we see in the modern construction industry can be explained by *transaction cost theory*. Profits in construction are no longer achieved by having the cleverest construction method or the cheapest supply of resources or the cleverest employment policies. These are all associated with *production costs*. Profits now lurk in the other major cost arena – transaction costs. All transactions in the construction process incur a cost associated with information and communication, as well as time and effort spent on the initiation and completion of a service exchange. Project solutions that minimize the total sum of these transaction costs will outperform competitors. Traditionally, the hierarchical organization has provided a mechanism for minimizing transaction costs because of the use of co-ordination mechanisms and control. However, modern information and communication systems such as the Internet can greatly reduce the transaction costs associated with information transfer. This applies to internal transactions using intranets as well as external transactions using secure Internet environments. So, it is perhaps no surprise to see partnering appearing high on peoples' agenda. One other feature we see associated with reducing costs of transactions is the advent of greater continuity between the design, construction and operation of buildings. Design-and-build and design-build-and-operate procurement systems are able to exploit reduced transaction costs because information and communication systems are put in place that allow for continuity.

Trust and virtuality

Wigand (1997) argues that '... trust and efficient information and communication systems foster market or cooperative forms of task completion'. However, the key point here is that firms cannot begin to exploit the benefits of Internet technology until some basis of trust is established. The question of trust becomes more important in the virtual world than in the real world. Handy (1995) posits the apparent paradox that 'the more virtual the organization, the more its people need to meet in person'. Ratnasingham (1998) contends that 'virtuality requires trust to make it work. Technology alone is not enough'. The idea of partnering in construction is discussed in *Trusting the Team* (Bennett and Jayes, 1995) where the characteristics of good partnering are described:

> The free and open exchange of information is an important characteristic of good partnering. Careful consideration needs to be given at each management level to the kind of information that should be made available to whom. A closely related feature of good practice is to work on the basis of open book costing. The essential principle is not to keep secrets from each other about the subject of the partnering arrangement. On the other hand it is important to respect the status of confidential information.

Not only is open book costing involved here, though – open book know-how, methods and technology may be involved in IT-based partnering.

Before developing a framework for Internet collaboration we need to get a firm understanding of what we mean by trust, of which the more common concern of security forms only a part. Trust can be described as 'the willingness of a party to be vulnerable to the actions of another party, based on the expectation that the other party will perform a particular action important to the trustor, irrespective of the ability to monitor or control that other party' (Mayer *et al.*, 1995). A trusting relationship obviates the need for many of the contractual control mechanisms often encountered in construction – retaining such control mechanisms destroys the opportunity of reduced transaction costs.

In this chapter, trust embraces both the sociological issues and technological issues. Failures of Internet security in the commercial world, time and again, are not the failure of technology but of people who abuse it. Firms involved in transactions need to consider (a) the technological issues that form the basis of trusting a trading partner and of being trusted, and (b) the wider issues of trust concerning the exposure to risk through the sharing of information.

Security and the Internet

For electronic commerce over the Internet, Ratnasingham (1998) puts forward a definition of security that embraces the concept of trust:

> Electronic commerce security in this context can thus be defined as a protection of an information resource from the threats and risks in the *Integrity*,

Confidentiality, *Authenticity*, *Non-Repudiation*, *Availability* and *Access Control* of the electronic transactions transmitted via telecommunications based systems ... and, more importantly ... the *reliability* of the trading parties.

Six threats concern trading organizations' competences in exchanging secure information. Construction organizations may fail to understand the security risks involved and jeopardize not only their own information but that of other partners. The last of these threats concerns the opportunistic behaviour of the trading partner, which is far less easy to resolve from a technological perspective. Before looking at each of these threats in turn it is instructive to examine the kind of security breaches encountered on the Internet. The Internet itself has evolved with little attention to security issues.

The lower-layer TCP/IP architecture used for the Internet is broadcast in nature. As a result, it is possible for any machine on the Internet that lies along a path between two communicating parties (an example being a service provider) to eavesdrop on traffic as it passes. This allows eavesdroppers to ascertain passwords and read the content of passed messages.

None of the systems used in the TCP/IP architecture provides any form of *authentication*. This means that it is virtually impossible to accurately determine whether the address of a data packet is genuine or not. One system can readily impersonate another system and it can be difficult to track down the identity of a fraudulent user.

Although some simple checksums are used to authenticate the contents of packets sent over the Internet, it is easy to circumvent these error-detection systems. This weakness allows the content of packets to be modified without the knowledge of sender or recipient.

Security is an issue for information in transit over the Internet and information stored on firms' own networks that have become visible to the outside world. These problems manifest themselves in several ways.

- *Eavesdropping* – This kind of activity may involve the theft of critical information as well as the theft of services normally limited to subscribers. Often, the simple knowledge that a transaction has taken place can be used against one or both of the parties involved. Tracking exchanges on the Internet can provide competitors with key market information. This is probably the most widespread form of eavesdropping in the commercial world and constitutes an invasion of an organization's privacy.
- *Password sniffing* – Today the process of hacking passwords is achieved not by a trial and error process but by the use of systematic methods for retrieving stored password data on poorly protected systems. The use of increasingly stronger cryptographic algorithms is likely to make password sniffing a more prevalent method.

- *Data modification* – The ability to change the content of information during a transaction presents a number of threats. Drawing information can be tampered with, producing erroneous design specifications, financial transactions can be altered with the modification of the payee on an electronic check.
- *Spoofing* – This elaborate form of theft on the Internet involves masquerading as a legitimate trading partner. By setting up a storefront, the unscrupulous party can elicit credit card numbers, passwords and collect payments from unsuspecting consumers.
- *Repudiation* – This is the electronic equivalent of the bounced cheque. If one party reneges on an agreement after a transaction, the other trading partner may have to pay for the cost of the transaction processing without benefiting from the transaction.

Dimensions of electronic security

What do we mean by electronic commerce security? There are seven different dimensions that should be considered in a security strategy (Table 6.1).

Table 6.1 Multifaceted view of electronic security.

Dimension	Description	Security measure
Authorization	The system should only allow authorized uses of the system by authorized users.	Digital signatures and public key certificates.
Authentication	The system should allow verification that parties to an electronic transaction are who they say they are.	Digital signatures and public key certificates.
Confidentiality	Communications between the transacting parties should not be visible to others. This confidentiality protects proprietary information and deters theft of information services.	Virtual private networks; data encryption.
Data integrity	The data sent in a transaction should not be capable of modification in transit or during storage (i.e. when on host machines).	Virtual private networks; data encryption; check sums.
Availability	The system should allow convenient access to services by legitimate users (possibly including mobile users in the construction context).	Secure remote mobile login systems.
Nonrepudiation	Neither of the parties involved in a transaction should be able to deny having participated in a transaction after the event.	Digital signatures and public key certificates.
Selective application of services	The system may be required to hide from view part of a transaction while part of the transaction is visible to the transacting party.	

Encryption concepts

Encryption is the security measure used to conceal the content of a message during a transaction. A readable message, known as a cleartext message, becomes unreadable to eavesdroppers when the content of a message is encrypted. Encryption (or scrambling) is achieved using a key. In *symmetric* cryptography the same key can be used to unscramble the message. This provides confidentiality of information but does little to ensure the integrity of the data and does not allow authentication of the parties involved. Another disadvantage of symmetric systems is that they often involve the large-scale distribution of the shared key. Inevitably the longer a single key is used and the more widespread its use the weaker the security system provided by the system using the key. Figure 6.1 shows the process of encryption and decryption in a symmetric system.

To meet the security requirements of electronic commerce a cryptographic method based on *asymmetric* keys is required. Otherwise known as the public key method, it involves the use of two distinct keys:

- *Private key* – This is kept secret by the holder and represents the identity of the owner.
- *Public key* – This is made available to the world.

The two mathematically linked keys are used in combination, as shown in Figure 6.2. Because of the inefficiency of most public key systems, signatures are often used in conjunction with a message digest, as shown in the figure.

Using the public key system, the private key, since it is an entity known only to the key owner, can be used as a form of digital signature. Thus, if a message is encrypted using an individual's private key, it can be assumed that the message was signed directly by the user. One disadvantage of the public key method is the increased

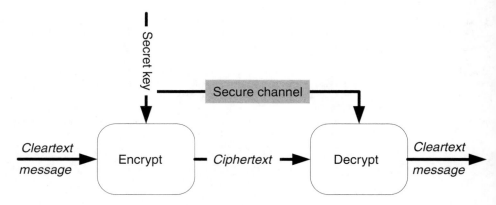

Fig. 6.1 Symmetric key system (based on Bhimani, 1996).

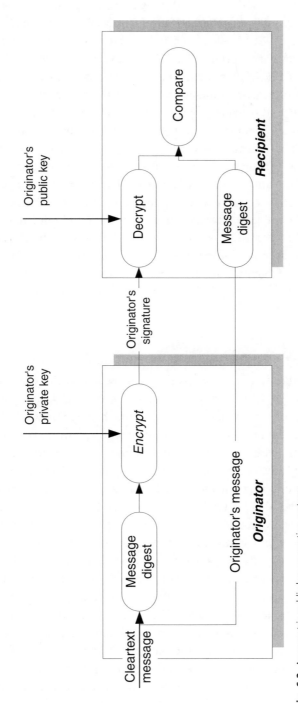

Fig. 6.2 Asymmetric public key encryption systems.

computational load incurred when encrypting and decrypting messages. As a result, both symmetric and public key methods are often used in combination.

With regard to the World Wide Web two different standards are currently competing for supremacy for securing HTTP (hypertext transfer protocol) transactions. The first of these is HTTPS, an amalgam of HTTP and secure socket layers (SSL) used in Netscape products providing network-level security. This was first introduced by Netscape in 1994 and provides security just about the TCP layer. It uses a combination of public key and symmetric cryptosystems. Client authentication is optional in this system. The short-term view on this design feature is that it was believed to be more important that consumers be aware of with whom they are conducting business than to give the merchants the same assurances. The competing standard is SHTTP (secure hypertext transfer protocol) which, in contrast to HTTPS, provides application-level security, confidentiality and integrity of data and authenticates the server and (optionally) the client. It is argued that SHTTP is more flexible than HTTPS, because it embeds security information within the existing HTTP protocol and supports a variety of algorithms and security measures. However, SHTTP is less widely adopted than HTTPS and it is more difficult to implement.

Firewalls

Construction organizations contemplating connecting their organization's local network to the Internet are understandably cautious about security implications. Firewalls provide a way of controlling the flow of traffic between networks. However, it is worth remembering that most unauthorized activities on networks originate from internal users. Furthermore, business partners interacting across private networks also have the potential to take advantage of a network link. Thus firewalls may be used to separate departments, workgroups, divisions and business partners on an internal system as well as Internet traffic. Sheldon (1996) uses the analogy of the medieval moat to explain how firewalls operate, as shown in Figure 6.3. The defensive strategy involves the use of a perimeter defence system of moats and walls. This effectively restricts the flow of traffic into and out of the castle to a series of choke points in the form of gatehouses and drawbridges. At these points it is possible to monitor and block access. Through each of the choke points, people with increased levels of trusted status are allowed to pass. Those with special credentials are allowed to enter the most highly fortified part of the castle, the castle keep, containing the most valuable assets. The market yard, on the perimeter of the castle, provides the public meeting place. This is where trading takes place, where local townspeople are free to exchange goods. This is directly analogous to a company's Web server or file transfer protocol (FTP) server, whereby outsiders can obtain information designed for general consumption.

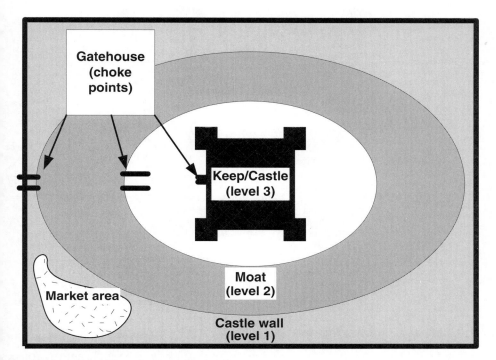

Fig. 6.3 Metaphor of firewall as a medieval castle.

Extending this analogy, it was customary for people to be strip-searched prior to meeting the king and queen. In times of particular political uncertainty, visitors would not have the opportunity to meet the king and queen directly. Instead, they would meet an agent. The agent would provide a proxy service, relaying the message to the royal dignitaries.

These approaches of strip-searching and proxy services are also employed in firewall systems used by firms connecting their networks to the Internet. Figure 6.4 shows the three distinct types of firewall system that are used.

Screening routers

A router is simply a dedicated computer that directs network traffic. Screening routers provide the strip-search method of security, connecting two networks at a choke point and performing packet filtering to control traffic between the two networks. They analyse every packet of information passing through it, looking at high-level address information, including the address of a computer, its internet protocol (IP) address, and the types of connection being used (e.g. Web, FTP, email). Implementation of a firewall system involves the definition of a set of rules that dictate how the filtering is

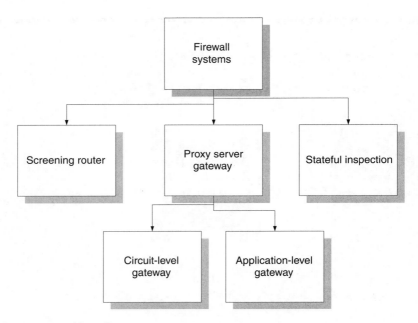

Fig. 6.4 Categories of firewall system.

undertaken. The robustness of a screening router is unlikely to be sufficient to protect network services when used in isolation because the filtering rules are often prone to error and vulnerable to penetration through unnoticed holes. Typically, screening routers are used in conjunction with another security measure.

Proxy server gateways

A proxy server acts as a middle-man, relaying requests from internal clients to external services on the Internet. A gateway is capable of operating at a higher level of the network protocol stack than a router. This enables them to carry out more sophisticated monitoring and traffic control. There are two types of proxy server, the circuit-level gateway and the application-level gateway.

The circuit-level gateway is generally used to connect trusted internal users to the Internet. It provides a controlled network connection between internal and external systems. One of the security risks associated with connecting networks to the Internet is that the internal network becomes more visible. Hackers are able to monitor network traffic and obtain information about individual computer identities. The proxy service changes the IP address of the client packets, concealing the identity of the internal system and providing only the identity of the proxy server.

The application-level gateway, in addition to providing the proxy service features, is also capable of providing extensive packet analysis. It goes beyond simply assessing

IP addresses with the analysis of data contained in the packets. Such a proxy service would provide a firewall capability for different protocols such as FTP (file transfer), HTTP (Web services) and SMTP (email). One of the disadvantages of such screening processes is the inevitable drop in performance. This is one reason why the alternative of stateful inspections is increasingly being used.

Stateful inspection technique

Instead of examining the contents of each packet, the stateful inspection technique looks at the bit pattern and compares this with packets that are already known to be trusted. When an internal user makes a request to the Internet, the server remembers things about the original request including the source and destination address. This process is known as 'saving the state'. When the responding system provides a return packet, the saved state information enables the server to determine whether the packet should be allowed or not. One of the disadvantages of the stateful inspection technique is that it does not conceal the IP address of the internal user. However, it does greatly reduce the latency of response due to the more selective filtering process.

Firewall policies

No amount of sophisticated firewall technology can overcome the need for a good firewall policy. Any weakness in the policy or in the ability to enforce a policy will expose firms to the risk of attacks from intruders. The most effective firewall policy from a security point of view is one that does not allow any traffic flow at all. However, such restrictive practices may backfire, causing internal users to go around firewalls and access the Internet through personal modems. A common firewall policy is to block all traffic and then allow specific services on a case-by-case basis. However, such a policy may be difficult to manage with a large number of rules having to be defined for screening-routers.

Sheldon (1996) lists a number of points that should form part of a firewall policy:

- All network traffic passing to and from the Internet must pass through the company firewall. Traffic should be filtered to allow only authorized packets to pass.
- The firewall system should never be used for general-purpose file storage or for running programs. It should be designed to be expendable in the case of attack.
- No passwords or internal addresses should be allowed to cross the firewall.
- Any public services (Web servers or FTP servers) should be put on the outside of the firewall.

- Use a replication scheme for any public system so that information can be automatically copied over a secure channel to restore the public system.

Virtual private networks

Internet security involves more than simply putting up a firewall to protect a corporate Internet from the great outside. What about the security of information in transit? To date, the vulnerability of this data passing through a public network such as the Internet has deterred many organizations from going down this path. Instead, they have persisted with corporate information networks based on the principle of exclusion. Proprietary protocols, supporting proprietary applications running over wide-area leased lines have been the established way of working for construction contractors. Having recognized the potential of an Internet-style network, many companies are now investigating the possibilities of redesigning their applications and data architectures along these lines. But such intranet systems remain costly private networks, with all the leasing costs that are associated with this. Is there a secure way of using a public infrastructure like the Internet? Virtual private networks (VPNs) are the next stage in security evolution following on from firewall technology. The encryption technology discussed so far provides a way of encrypting package data (the payload), although the destination and source address remain visible. With virtual private networks, entire IP packets are encapsulated, including the address information. Given this level of security, the Internet then takes on the form of a completely private network (hence the name). The objective of VPNs is to provide corporations with a communications highway for sharing proprietary information with employees and nonproprietary information with clients. Between these two extremes, it also enables the sharing of selected information with trading partners.

Unfortunately, VPNs are currently in a state of flux with various competing standards being put forward. Among them are Cisco's Layer 2 Forwarding (L2F), Microsoft and Cisco's combined Layer 2 Tunneling Protocol (L2TP), and the Internet Engineering Task Force's (IETF) Encapsulated Security Payload (ESP) protocol. It is clear that in the long term there is only room for one VPN solution as an industry standard. The successful standard should be flexible enough to be easily set up by users, have minimal performance latency, minimal overhead and should be ubiquitous.

Partnering and trust

Up to this point in the chapter we have restricted our attention to only one element of trust – that area of trust concerned with our ability and that of trading partners to safeguard information in an electronic environment. However, the issue of trust of greatest concern to construction organizations is not that of theft by outsiders but rather the opportunistic exploitation of our own information by a trading partner. As we have seen, new trading practices such as partnering promise greatly reduced transaction costs. But they also involve exposure of business processes and information. In the virtual environment, greater visibility brings about greater vulnerability. How do we safeguard our organization against this?

Partnering can exist between any combination of clients, contractors, specialist contractors and consultants. Its primary goal is to improve productivity, and information technology and communications are increasingly the stimulus that prompts such partnerships. Bennett and Jayes (1995) define partnering as follows:

> Partnering is a management approach used by two or more organisations to achieve business objectives by maximising the effectiveness of each participant's resources. The approach is based on mutual objectives, an agreed method of problem resolution and an active search for continuous measurable improvements. Partnering can be based on a single project (project partnering) but greater benefits are available when it is based on a long term commitment (strategic partnering).

The rationale for partnering given by Bennett and Jayes (1995) interestingly makes no mention of the significance of information and communications technology, but suggests that

> The largest benefits arise in design and management processes. This is because these rely on the communication of information, and as partnering encourages people to work together, they become significantly more efficient at understanding each other and so, for example, fewer words are needed to explain an idea fully.

Their study found that improvements in productivity that arise from designers, managers and clients working together for several years range from 50% to 200%. The likely productivity improvements in direct construction activities were unlikely to be of the same magnitude, typically being between 5% and 20%. Again, this reinforces the evidence that it is the transaction costs that dominate the design and management processes, and it is no surprise that information technology is leveraging this kind of return.

The relevance of trust in this context can be seen in another definition (Cummings and Bromiley, 1996):

> Trust is the calculation of the likelihood of future cooperation and is a defining feature of virtual cooperation. As trust declines, people are increasingly unwilling to take risks and demand greater protection against the probability of betrayal. . . .

Relationships are never static, be it romantic, manager–employee or trading partners involved in electronic commerce. Trust is therefore complex, multifaceted and changing. Shapiro *et al.* (1992) mapped out an evolutionary model of trust between two trading parties from observations of firms. They observed three stages of maturity:

- *Calculus-based trust* – This state of trust arises from the rewards of being trusted and the threat that if trust is violated a firm's reputation can be hurt through a trading partner's network. The threat of punishment (deterrence-based trust) is likely to be a more significant motivator than the promise of reward. Calculus-based trust is firmly established in a rational perspective of self-interest.
- *Knowledge-based trust* – In this stage of trust development, there is a high-level knowledge of the trading partner's business. The truster is able to predict the behaviour of the trustee as a result of the information derived out of the relationship.
- *Identification-based trust* – This constitutes the most mature form of business trust. It relies on the development of empathy and common values with the other trading partner. Over the passage of time, the trading partner is able to act as an agent for the other. Typically, their combined effort involves working on common tasks. In contrast to calculus-based trust, identification-based trust is founded more on the social perspective of moral duty.

Figure 6.5 illustrates the developmental trust model. A follow-up study by Lewicki and Bunker (1996) found it to be a true reflection of business behaviour. Trust was created at the deterrence-based level provided there was a credible threat of

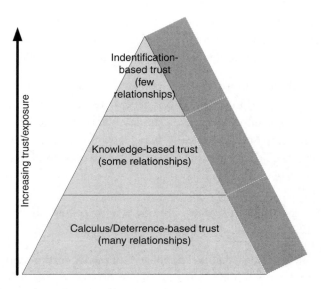

Fig. 6.5 The evolution of trust (based on Shapiro *et al.*, 1992).

punishment of failing to co-operate. At the second level of knowledge-based trust, trust was assured provided people's dispositions were well known and their behaviour could be reliably predicted. At the third level of identification-based trust, trust is seen to be working when both partners are acting in a way that considers joint gains, and the needs and desires of both are taken into account.

So what are the implications of trust for construction firms contemplating virtual trading? Nohria and Eccles (1992) identified some of the obstacles to the formation of trust in this context:

- The lack of co-presence in time and space.
- The lack of entire human bandwidth (sight, hearing, touch) during remote interactions.
- The absence of opportunities for interruption, feedback and learning.

The clear message here is that prior familiarity is an essential component of trust formation. Moreover, of paramount importance are shared past experiences and an expectation of a common future. No amount of technological wizardry can bypass this need (Walther, 1995).

Benefits of trust

So what are the benefits of trust? Beyond the reduction in transaction costs, trusting relationships will inevitably reduce the adversarial nature of the construction process. An industry previously reliant on contracts and claims to protect firms' interests is now looking to reduce the burden of legal fees and unnecessary conflict. In an environment of trust, firms will be able to enter into partnerships that would otherwise have been deemed impractical. The considerable search costs and duplication of effort can be reduced through the liberating effect of open standards and Internet technology.

KEY POINTS FROM THIS CHAPTER

- The Internet will make the processes and information of firms more visible. Trust therefore becomes a key issue.

- The Internet allows firms to significantly reduce transaction costs through partnering. The increased use of partnering also increases the importance of trust.

- Rather than reducing the need for face-to-face communication the Internet may actually increase it – as firms attempt to establish and maintain trust.

- Trust can only be placed in collaborating firms if there is a level of confidence in the security measures being adopted.

- Virtual private networks will greatly increase the level of security enjoyed by collaborating firms using the Internet.

7

Creating trade

Questions addressed in this chapter

- Is e-commerce just about electronic purchasing or is it something more?

- What are the stages of buying in the construction industry and are they any different from any other industry?

- What part does EDI (electronic data interchange) have in the trading process – and does this rely on the Internet?

- How do intranets and extranets fit into the e-commerce picture?

- What are the opportunities offered by new agent technologies?

Our early experiences using the World Wide Web may not have enlightened us but rather blinkered our vision of its possibilities, in just the same way that people were deterred by computers following earlier experiences with arithmetic machines and punch cards. (Cummings and Bromiley, 1996)

Dodo strategy

Clients do not sit at computers trawling the Web looking for a suitable architect, nor are they ever likely to. Building specifiers do not rummage through lists of manufacturers' Web sites looking for the ideal product. Why? Because unlike the consumer market, in the business-to-business market sellers come to the buyers not vice versa. Commerce revolves around a push model, not a pull model. So what possible use could the Internet be if Web technology revolves around this push model? Is it anything more than an endless electronic highstreet of virtual shopfronts? The Web is evolving at a formidable pace to a point where it will bear only superficial similarities to the one we have encountered to date. A dramatic shift towards a push model will be made possible through the combined use of machine-readable Web sites and agent technology. This chapter takes a forward look at this technology and notes that some industries are already exploiting this new generation of Internet technology. Construction firms stuck in the pull model mindset will soon find that their seemingly high-tech e-commerce strategy is a dodo. For some, this chapter may be uncomfortable reading.

Broad view of e-commerce

Mention the word e-commerce and many business managers think about buying and selling over the Internet. For this reason it is often thought of as irrelevant to the business-to-business trading that occurs in construction. E-commerce is not just a trading system, nor is it just a marketing mechanism. In formulating an Internet strategy, construction professionals need to clarify the role of e-commerce and how it can be used to support the total delivery of a service or product.

E-commerce is given to mean many different things in the business community. A broad definition given by Zwass (1996) describes it 'as the sharing of information, maintaining business relationships, and conducting business transactions by means of telecommunications networks'. Applying this definition we see that e-commerce applies to a wide range of activities in the construction process. It also embraces the sharing of business information within organizations. Four types of technology are converging to facilitate e-commerce:

- Electronic messaging – including fax and email.
- Sharing of corporate digital libraries for the purpose of collaborative working.
- Electronic document interchange and electronic funds transfer.
- Electronic publishing to enable marketing, advertising, sales and customer support.

Electronic document interchange is a technology that has developed independently of the Internet – although the Internet is increasingly being used to carry secure Internet transactions. EDI is used to support business-to-business interactions, allowing the settlement of payments between contractors and subcontractors. Unlike the consumer market in which transactions involve single product transactions, these financial transactions involve batch processing of payments. The Web has until now been directed at the electronic publishing opportunities in the commercial business-to-business context.

What is evident from questionnaire studies (Kalakota and Whinston, 1996) is that business managers tend to restrict their ideas of e-commerce to EDI or electronic publishing. The questions that construction firms must ask are: 'How should an Internet strategy be formulated to leverage e-commerce and support the total delivery process?' 'How can e-commerce be made to impact on business up and down the value chain?'

Stages of the buying process

Whatever stage of the construction supply chain we look at, we can see buyer/seller transactions that follow a particular sequence of steps. Indeed, for the overall procurement process there are very well defined steps. However, we should not forget that behind the apparently unique façade of construction procurement runs a more generic sequence of stages common to all forms of trading. These are similar to the kind encountered in the consumer market, but differ markedly in complexity. Various models based on consumer buying behaviour (CBB) all incorporate seven common stages:

1. *Need identification* – Describes the point where a buyer becomes conscious of an unmet need: a client realizes they have insufficient space; a heating engineer recognizes a need to provide a cooling capacity; or a contractor recognizes the need to recruit a form-work gang.
2. *Product brokering* – At this stage the buyer sets about obtaining information about what product or service is available to satisfy their need. A client might be choosing a type of procurement; an architect might be selecting a particular type of wall cladding. The result of this search is the *consideration set* of products. In procurement, the details of a contractor's proposed design or construction solutions issued in a tender bid provide the consideration set.
3. *Merchant brokering* – With the consideration set from the preceding stage at hand, the buyer gleans merchant-specific information in order to determine who to buy the product from. This involves the evaluation of information on warranty, availability, liquidity, delivery time and reputation. In the building procurement process, this brokering process may take the form of a tender list to enable initial screening. The tender thus provides a single method for product brokering and merchant brokering.
4. *Negotiation* – Unlike the consumer market that is generally controlled by fixed prices, most commercial transactions involve complex negotiations varying in duration. The negotiation of quality, cost and time are integral to the buying process in construction transactions.
5. *Payment and settlement* – The delivery and payment options may significantly affect the choice of product or broker. Execution of payments is increasingly

Table 7.1 The scope of XML and agents in e-commerce

Buying process stage	Electronic data interchange (EDI)	Extensible markup language (XML)	Agents	Bar coding
Need identification			✓	
Product brokering		✓	✓	
Merchant brokering		✓	✓	
Negotiation			✓	
Payment and settlement	✓	✓	✓	
Supply chain management	✓	✓	✓	✓
Service and evaluation		✓	✓	✓

being undertaken electronically using EDI technology. This reduces the cost and errors associated with data re-entry as well as minimizing the time and security risks associated with a transaction.

6. *Supply chain management* – Effective trading allows the maintenance of minimal inventories in order to minimize inventory overheads, damage during storage and product obsolescence.
7. *Product service and evaluation* – Concerns the post-purchase support of customers and products as well as vital feedback on the overall buying experience of the customer. The advent of client-partnering increases the importance of this final stage, providing a continuous trading loop.

To what extent can a virtual value chain supplant a physical value chain in this sequence? Only one of these stages – that of payment and settlement – has been explored to any significant extent in the construction industry. The construction industry around the world continues to equate e-commerce with EDI. Looking at the various stages of the buyer–seller relationship we see that EDI covers only a very narrow spectrum of the overall process. Moreover, although EDI offers a way of pushing forward the productivity frontier, only by examining some of the other stages of the trading cycle can we really exploit strategic business benefits.

Table 7.1 shows the coverage of EDI and other competing technologies. In the following sections we explore each of these areas in turn. The complementarity between markup language (XML) and agent technology threatens to displace EDI as we know it. We will explore why this is the case and the implications for those involved in the implementation of an e-commerce strategy.

Electronic data interchange in construction

Electronic data interchange facilitates the application-to-application transfer of business data between or within companies. These transfers typically include the exchange of quotations, purchase orders and invoices as discrete electronic messages. An EDI message is not dissimilar to an email, containing a string of text-based information. But there are some key differences:

- EDI messages are designed to be read by computers, not people. They allow one computer's input to be provided by another's output.
- EDI messages, being designed for computer exchange, rely on the use of a preset format, allowing accounting and inventory software to process the data.
- EDI messages can be carried over a number of different types of network including the public telephone network, the Internet and by value-added networks (VANs).
- EDI messages exploit security features of electronic transfer not possible using paper-based systems. Digital signatures and digital time stamps provide incontrovertible evidence that an authorized sender has confirmed payment at a particular point in time.

EDI technology originally evolved independently of the Internet, with the involvement of third-party VANs providing two fundamental roles: (a) the secure handling and control of EDI transactions and (b) the transmission of EDI transactions. Originally, commercial Wide Area Networks (WANs) were used to carry these messages but, increasingly, VANs are using the Internet for secure transactions. As a result, their value-added contribution is increasingly related to the handling rather than the transmission element of EDI. The advent of Virtual Private Networks (VPNs) will increasingly enable construction firms to undertake EDI transactions without reliance on third-party VANs.

There are two preeminent standards currently in use for EDI exchange, EDIFACT (EDI in Administration, Commerce and Transport) and ANSI X.12. In addition to generic standards, considerable work has been undertaken in the construction industry to produce standards applicable to the particular type of documents encountered in construction. Two organizations in the UK, EDICON (EDI in Construction) and CITE (Construction Industry Trading Electronically) have made considerable progress towards implementing an industry standard for many types of document including:

- drawing information
- tender preparation documents
- specifications
- bills of quantities
- contract documents
- project management.

Those organizations currently using EDI are making considerable cost savings. EDI eliminates expensive document handling. It also reduces rekeying of data with a consequent reduction in processing time, errors and effort. Duyshart (1997) quotes the savings of RJR Nabisco who have estimated that traditional processing of paper purchase orders costs the company about $70 per order, but by processing an EDI purchase order this cost can be reduced to 93 cents.

Plug-and-play organizations using XML

The adoption of EDI in the construction industry continues to be slow and piecemeal in nature. The infrastructure for using EDI has been in place for over a decade and yet construction firms have failed to grasp the nettle. Why is this? Traditional EDI is complex and expensive, particularly for smaller firms who are often reluctant partners in an integration process. The expense arises from the continued use of proprietary networks. The brittle syntax of EDI also necessitates a process of custom integration between each pair of trading partners. This is what Glushko *et al.* (1999) describe as the 'pairwise tyranny through which big companies impose proprietary message formats on smaller companies'.

An overarching feature of e-commerce to date has been the overemphasis on system-level rather than business-level integration. Interconnection between trading partners has been achieved by the laborious integration of business systems interfaces, all of which differ markedly from one another. EDI has become a black box that is only accessible to information technologists. Many organizations now acknowledge the value of using a document-based approach to information exchange. This approach relies on documents that people as well as computers can understand: familiar documents like catalogues, purchase orders, tender documents and specifications.

Extensible markup language (XML) is the language that makes this approach possible. The ability to use XML to convey EDI messages over the Internet offers the prospect of much lower costs and a flexibility appropriate to all sizes of construction firm. XML will eliminate the need for custom interfaces for every trading relationship between customer and supplier.

Because XML is interpretable by both humans and computers (and agents), XML documents provide a progressive path to business automation that can easily be assimilated by smaller firms. Many of the costs and risk involved with system integration can be bypassed.

eCo System project

A large number of industries are already banding together to exploit the benefits of Internet-based e-commerce for business-to-business trading. Perhaps the most important cross-industry work is that of the 500 member worldwide consortium known as the CommerceNet Consortium. Conceived in 1996, their aim was to bring about open

Internet commerce. The eCo System architecture that has arisen from the consortium's work is based on XML. It enables companies to communicate over the Internet using self-defining XML business documents. These documents, known as business interface definitions (BIDs), are posted on the Web and tell trading partners what documents to use when making use of a particular service. For example, a BID might be used to allow a customer to submit a purchase order or obtain schedule listings.

Central to the operation of the eCo System framework is the existence of an electronic library of documents known as the Common Business Language (CBL). This public collection of templates can easily be altered and tailored to the requirements of individual companies. The library includes message templates for other established EDI standards including the ANSI X.12, Open Trading Protocol (OTP – developed by a consortium of banking and technology companies to help with the specification of information requirements for payments, receipts, delivery and customer support), and the Open Buying on the Internet (OBI) standard. The ability to map any such Internet standard to a particular CBL, means that firms can quickly define their own business interface and trade with whoever they wish electronically (Figure 7.1).

The document-centred approach used on the eCo System requires standardization

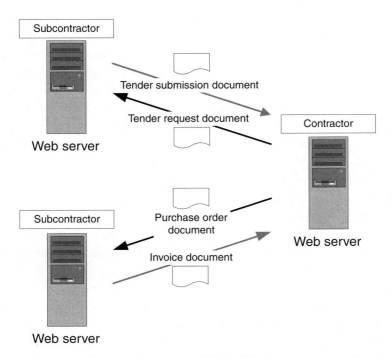

Fig. 7.1 Use of the eCo Server concept to generate XML-based exchange documents (based on Glushko *et al.*, 1999).

on the structure, content and ordering of information used in XML documents. How this information is then processed and what actions result is irrelevant, these being determined by the trading partner. The use of common business elements enables the reuse of business components and greatly accelerates the speed with which standards can be assimilated.

As we have seen earlier, the Internet as it stands is inadequate, because information is not semantically encoded (HTML is used to express appearance but not meaning). As a result, search agents and software agents have to use whatever ingenious methods can be devised to elicit content. Imagine an Internet environment in which every change in your company's Web site, every product change, every price alteration and every schedule modification is instantaneously and automatically relayed to customers and trading partners – but not just in an ad hoc way. Rather, it is an environment where every prospective buyer is able to simultaneously and continuously compare product and service offerings. The use of a richer markup language such as XML makes this a possibility.

Software agents

The full potential of e-commerce has yet to be realized. Humans are still used extensively throughout buying processes in construction. The prospect of automated buying seems a long way off. But software agents have all the characteristics of a technology capable of greatly reducing the humans' effort involved in many aspects of e-commerce. Their usage extends well beyond EDI, to encompass the whole buying process from need identification to customer support. Software agents (often referred to simply as agents) are small computer programs that are able to act independently on the Internet. Think of the analogy of agents working for the FBI. Specialized agents may be home-based (e.g. at the Pentagon) and given specific tasks, such as monitoring radio broadcasts from an unstable country. They may be instructed to look out for specific events like political changes or signs of popular unrest. Software agents serve an identical type of function on the Internet. Provided with specific behavioural instructions they are able to monitor information on the Internet, interpret that information and even make decisions about it. But FBI agents are not just home based. To obtain *rich* information they have to be located where the events are happening, picking up daily information on some remote island of unrest. They have to be mobile and remote from the host organization (and as such capable of acting autonomously). An exact counterpart to this idea can be found in software agents. Known as mobile agents, these agents can be sent out to populate the Internet, interrogating information at the exact location where it resides. This is very different from the traditional method of obtaining information over the Internet, whereby a host computer carries out queries (a conversation) to and fro across the Internet. The key characteristics of agents are:

- They operate continuously – turn off your computer and the agent continues to function.
- They are personalized – the behaviour of the agent can be designed to satisfy the specific needs of the user.
- They are semiautonomous – once provided with certain parameters they are able to operate independently, collecting and disseminating information in a responsive manner.

Construction firms make money from good buying practices. The ability to secure low-cost supplies may be the principal value adding contribution that a contractor makes to the construction process. Perhaps they are able to secure good prices by buying in bulk or by establishing a trusting relationship with a specific supplier. Negotiation takes place by an artful process of negotiation. Are Internet agents really capable of replacing this capability? Do construction firms want to move from an imperfect market of buyers and sellers to a world of perfect information and software agents? After all, an imperfect market provides just the environment for firms to make money. The reality is that human involvement will continue to be a fundamental part of the buying process, but agents will be an increasingly useful tool in their armoury. Rather than simply pushing forward the operational efficiency boundary, agent technology will enable firms to gain distinct market advantages. The ability to design their own agents, with their own information gathering and negotiation strategies, will provide firms with a method of buying that is distinct from the competition.

Agent technology is already being used in the consumer market. But, given the increasing sophistication of the technology, it is possible to envisage a rapid progression into the business-to-business arena of e-commerce. Imagine an agent system for procuring stone cladding:

An agent is used by a building firm to monitor their own stockpile of cladding and co-operates with another agent monitoring the demand side. The *monitoring agent* alerts the supplier when available domestic sources become depleted and a buying agent is launched. The *buying agent* then collects information on vendors from around the world, gathering information on price, availability, lead time and various other properties relating to the product and the merchant. The buying agent negotiates the price with the merchant agents. The purchase is confirmed after a number of renegotiations, with confirmation from the human buyer.

This scenario seems like science fiction. But for the consumer market, an Internet world populated by agents is already becoming a reality. For the construction industry, as encoding becomes more effective and Web information becomes more machine readable, this scenario may not be so far in the future.

Need identification using agents

Agent monitors can be used to identify when a new need arises. Imagine for example an agent used by a developer to monitor the business space needs of a past client – Company X. The monitoring agent, instructed to monitor public on-line information such as employee numbers or liquidity ratio of Company X, following a long period of dormancy, is triggered into action when a significant change takes place. It then reports this change back to the developer. A design firm specializing in low-energy design might use agents to monitor product releases. A contractor using a favoured crane hire firm might use agents to alert them to more competitive rates from competing firms when a certain threshold is passed. Exactly this principle is being used by the booksellers Amazon.com to bring to the attention of customers new book releases. By carefully profiling the reading habits of past book customers, Amazon.com are able to alert customers to highly targeted information about new book releases in their area of interest, or by their favourite author.

Product and merchant brokering

Agents are able to assimilate complex information about products and brokers to help buyers in the critical evaluation of options. Tete-a-tete (on line at ecommerce.media.mit.edu/tete-a-tete) is an example of an on-line agent that provides an intelligent search environment for buyers. It helps buyers to articulate their needs and in so doing filter out unsuitable options. Comparison techniques based on multi-attribute utility theory are used by this agent to recommend complex products.

Another ingenious software agent known as Firefly (on line at www.firefly.com) uses word-of-mouth recommendation systems called 'collaborative filtering' to help with product selection. This system is able to recognize buyers with similar tastes or requirements. These are identified as the 'nearest neighbours'. The system then recommends products the neighbour rated highly but which the buyer has yet to try. Firefly is currently being use to offer recommendations on consumer products such as music and books.

Negotiation

The Tete-a-tete agent developed at MIT's Media Lab in the USA is one of the more sophisticated negotiation agents. Unlike other negotiation agents it is able to negotiate over issues other than price, including warranties, service contracts and loan options. The system uses merchant-owned sales agents and consumer-owned shopping agents to participate in the negotiation. Because the system integrates product and brokering characteristics it is possible to readily identify a suitable product configuration.

Service and evaluation

The Villa Wega demonstration project undertaken at the University of Karlskrona in Sweden (Akkermans *et al.*, 1996) shows the immense possibilities of using software agents for building monitoring and energy conservation. The project looked at the issue of load balancing on the electric grid and the energy savings based on smart devices in the home. It operates at two levels:

1. *The smart home* – The system makes use of the Echelon LonWork building control protocol that enables separate devices in the building to talk to one another. An active badge system is used to track people as they move through a building. The active badges, worn by the occupant, relay information to a badge server agent via control panels located in the rooms. Various interacting agents including the personal comfort agent, the room agent and the environment parameter agent pick up information from the active badge and various sensors. They then activate actuators around the building and report information to the house agent. The house agent is able to consult the overall goals and constraints of the building management system and resolve any local conflicts. The local intelligence obtained at the home level is then used to enable load balancing.
2. *Load balancing* – Using local information provided by house agents, the electrical utility provider is able to balance the demand for energy, avoiding costly electricity production. This in turn means lower bills for the customer. Such information can be)trawled from many thousands of homes connected to an electricity utility. The utility makes use of the electrical grid not just as a means of carrying electricity but as a way of carrying information (including agents) as well. By a technology known as mains signalling, information can be transmitted using the Internet TCP/IP standard. This eliminates the need to put in dedicated Internet connections to monitor building performance. Agents are not just used for reporting and optimization, however. They are also used in the negotiation stage to identify the most cost-effective source of electricity. A bidding process between a utility agent and a customer agent takes place over the electricity grid. Using this approach it is possible to instantaneously and continuously review the source of the electricity supplier.

The examples above illustrate the scope of agent technology in e-commerce. For some, they create a somewhat discomforting feeling of loss of control. But just how relevant is agent technology to the large-scale business-to-business environment? Does it form part of the plug-and-play concept of virtual enterprises discussed earlier? Certainly, agent technology is still in its infancy, but as we shall see in the following example, agent technology is starting to attract considerable interest in the manufacturing sector.

Commercial examples of agent-based e-commerce

Leaders in the manufacturing sector are pushing ahead vigorously with software agent technology. One prominent example is the SMART project run by the National Industrial Information Infrastructures Protocols (NIIIP) in the US (described by Jain and Singh, 1997). This project is focusing on the use of multi-agent systems in supply chains. Like construction, the manufacturing industry is distributed, involving a large number of autonomous commercial entities, all with different information systems. They also have to deal with the problems of failure and exceptions in physical processes and contractual arrangements. The proposed system takes into account three aspects of information structuring: (a) data integrity and flow, (b) organizational structure (how the parties relate to each other), and (c) how the autonomy of trading partners is preserved.

Underlying their system design is the concept of a *sphere of commitment*. A commitment is a relationship between a debtor and a creditor and the sphere of commitment (otherwise known as the SoCom) is the scope within which a commitment applies. A concrete SoCom is created when agents (of buyers and vendors) become engaged in such a realm. This model, based on legal reasoning, provides the kind of flexibility necessary to reflect the complexities of e-commerce between commercial trading partners. Jain and Singh (1997) describe in detail how this system operates using the example of a supply chain involving an air conditioning manufacturer that procures valves and hoses from two downstream suppliers. The example illustrates how the air-conditioning manufacturer is able to operate as a procurer in one relationship and a supplier in another (as creditors and debtors using their terminology). A particularly interesting feature of the system is that it deals with complex transactions where commitments are unfulfilled – a common issue in the construction industry. One example might be the late delivery of parts from a supplier. Because the agent technology embraces an understanding of 'process', the system is able to behave in a flexible way. If the delay is the result of a change in specification, the behaviour of the agent is different from a situation where the delay is caused by a supplier's failings.

Two key features also play a part in this e-commerce agent architecture. The first is the reliance on encoded information being present on the Internet. For this – read

XML! Another feature is the emergence of truly virtual stores that allow comparative shopping not just between products but between vendors. This entails the use of agents by the virtual store itself to assemble information from many vendors' web sites into one coherent system.

Identifying e-commerce applications

In order to explore the boundaries of e-commerce in an Internet strategy a planning framework is useful. Riggins and Rhee (1998) proposed the use of two variables that help to distinguish between the different application areas of e-commerce:

- *Location of users relative to system firewall* – A firewall is a system used to protect a company's network from unwelcome intruders via the Internet. Firewalls use a combination of hardware and software to police and restrict the flow of information between an organization's network and the Internet proper. Complex methods of tracking, monitoring and authentication are used to ensure that only authorized users get access to information. By providing outside access, many construction firms have helped to publicize their products and services via the World Wide Web. On-line catalogues, case studies and company details help to communicate the desired image of the company. At the other extreme, the intranet has helped many construction firms develop highly effective ways of reaching employees. Information such as schedules, contacts and diaries can be set up using low-cost software, with data entry by the individual involved.
- *Types of relationship affected* – The second variable that helps to explain e-commerce opportunities is the permanence of the relationship involved in information exchange. Interorganizational systems (IOS) can be developed to support relationships with existing trading partners or new trading partners. Malone *et al.* (1996) describe those that support existing relationships as technology-enhanced relationships. In the construction industry, these systems are likely to evolve in partnering relationships. Such systems arise where clients, contractors and consultants are seeking long-term benefits from an established working relationship: relationships in which the partners have established common exchange standards, skills mix and complementarity of resources. In the case of new trading partners, IOS systems provide technology-facilitated relationships. These are relationships that are only possible because of the new possibilities that arise from the Internet. Construction, by definition, concerns projects. As such, these projects, with a discrete beginning and end, bring together various contractors for a duration that is only as long as the project itself. The temporary nature of these relationships means that the systems required to support them are temporary as well – with participants joining and leaving at various stages. These temporary relationships

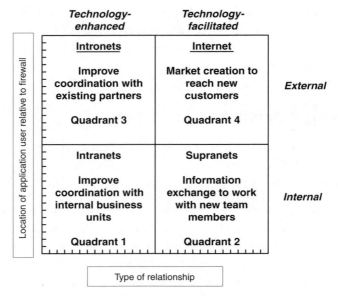

Fig. 7.2 Framework of e-commerce exploitation in construction.

make use of technology-facilitated relationships. Through them, virtual teams can arise, both within and outside of organizations.

Figure 7.2 shows a framework for identifying the various areas of e-commerce (adapted from the general business framework of Riggins and Rhee (1998)). The two dimensions of 'location of user relative to firewall' and 'type of relationship' create the four quadrants.

This matrix reveals the four domains of e-commerce. The domain in Quadrant 4 represents the Internet proper that provides access for everyone. The construction industry has demonstrated considerable interest in this area – the focus being on the capture of new clients. Typically, involvement in this area is the first stage of further involvement in net technologies. At the other extreme are intranets (Quadrant 1), providing a closed exchange environment, but founded on the same net standards. Again, this area has been well explored by many firms in construction, seeking to increase internal efficiencies.

By far the most unexplored applications of e-commerce in construction are in Quadrants 2 and 3. As building designs become more complex, manufacturing agility off-site becomes more significant. Furthermore, with a trend towards greater client focus, the dominance of any single contractor becomes less pronounced. We start to see the emergence of the hyperarchy or 'project ecosystem'. In character, this struc- ture differs fundamentally from the traditional forms of project organization. Rigid hierarchical structures are replaced by complex interlinking relationships. An example would be the design of an intelligent building where the specialist contractor may leapfrog the intermediary contractor, dealing directly with the client.

Extranets

The vast untapped area of net technologies encompassed by Quadrants 2 and 3 in Figure 7.2 represent what are collectively known as extranets. Extranets offer the possibility of filling the void that currently exists between Internet and intranet applications. They offer the possibility of creating true hyperarchies.

Two types of extranet

Extranets are collaborative networks that use Internet technology to enable trading partners to exchange information in one of two ways:

- providing controlled access to a portion of a company's intranet;
- establishing a common network linking trading partners.

Based on this distinction, we can define two types of extranet:

- *Intronets* – Trading partners are able to obtain controlled access to an initiator's information system behind an initiating trading partner's firewall. These are represented by Quadrant 2 in Figure 7.2.
- *Supronets* – Trading partners involved in the construction value chain share a common networked decision-support system using Web browser technology. These are largely represented by Quadrant 3.

Intronets

Users of an intronet are able to retrieve information maintained on an initiating partner's database, made visible via a Web browser. This provides the user with greater control over how the information is used. However, the initiator is able to determine the content and functionality.

Why would a contractor involved in a construction project volunteer to provide trading partners with access to part of their intranet system? One of the key motivations is the ability to lock trading partners into a symbiotic relationship. The intronet provides a means to reduce transaction costs for both parties. Furthermore, users move through a learning curve when using an initiator's intronet, making the switching costs to another partner more costly. Software providers and manufacturers involved in construction have recognized the strategic benefits of intronets. Companies such as Intergraph and AutoCAD have developed extensive component libraries available via the Internet to software users. Manufacturers are also providing digital catalogues online, either directly or via software providers. The rationale behind this effort is that specifiers are more likely to choose manufactured components that can be readily assimilated into their prototype CAD models.

An example of a successful intronet application in facilities management, described by Riggins and Rhee (1998), is the AllView system developed by Lucent. Lucent are a supplier of network and switching equipment to various telecommunications companies. As part of this role, they maintain a large archive of documentation relating to their client companies. These engineering documents include standard drawings, floor plans, equipment and network drawings of particular facilities. Many of these drawings include information provided by vendors in competition with Lucent. Historically, vendors wishing to bid for work on a contract of one of the telecommunications companies would have to approach the telecommunications company, who in turn would obtain relevant documents from Lucent. The documents would then be sent to the vendor as manual copies.

In 1995 Lucent developed AllView – a system that allowed users with a Web browser and accompanying plug-in to access the engineering documentation. This was initially developed to allow users in their own company to bid more efficiently. The Web system included a number of markup tools, allowing users to annotate and comment on the drawings. A facility was also put in place to allow documents to be changed and submitted as new versions. In 1995 there were 200 internal users, but by 1996 there were over 1000 users.

Lucent soon recognized the value-adding benefits of providing this capability to clients. It would enable internal operational efficiency for Lucent and provide greater customer satisfaction. Vendors bidding for work no longer needed to use Lucent as a go-between to access electronic drawings – electronic versions could be obtained directly via the telecommunications company tendering the work. Lucent benefited through the creation of an entirely new market in which it could determine price levels for various levels of support. In the construction industry, this type of manoeuvre of allowing open access to digital information is often resisted. Continued reliance on incomplete CAD models protects the originator of the information from intellectual piracy. However, it is clear that in the interest of clients, a more open strategy is required. Clients are increasingly recognizing electronic drawings as part of the delivered product (not just the building), and that any attempt to reduce the richness of this information during exchanges will only increase transaction costs.

Supronets

Supronets are developed by a consortium of organizations to increase efficiency and reduce the time involved in design and construction. Such systems have been developed to deal with single projects, but increasingly they are being used to enable a more permanent consortium structure to be used in more than one project. This greatly increases the returns on learning curves and hardware investment. The consortium sponsor and control the system, using groupware, project management and document management software. The greatest returns arise from the standardization of document and database templates used in interorganizational exchange. The more the trading partners become locked into a common supronet, the more protected their working methods become. The appeal of a such a consortium to a client, is not just the quality of the project, but the reassurance that transaction costs are being minimized.

One example of a supronet in the manufacturing industry is the Infotest Enhanced Product Realisation (EPR) Project (www.infotest.com). This case study project is designed to show how Internet technology can be used to enable seamless product development through the entire value chain, creating a true virtual organization. In addition to conventional Web technologies, the project made use of video conferencing, electronic whiteboarding, CAD/CAM, product data exchange and virtual work teams.

What direction are extranets likely to go in construction? Intronets are suited to organizations with a dominant role in the construction market – various international companies such as Bechtel, Foster Wheeler, Taylor Woodrow and Lend Lease would fall into this category. The main contractor is able to provide proprietary access for individual subcontractors accessing their intronet. The intronet provides a dependency relationship for the subcontractor as it enables reduced transaction costs. The same subcontractor contemplating participation in a competing bid would have to account for greater costs because of the absence of such an intronet. In terms of long-term strategic advantage intronets may offer greater potential than supranets. Supronets are easily mimicked, so that they rapidly become a common feature across the industry. In contrast, the proprietary nature of intronets will enable lead firms to enjoy a sustained advantage while reaping the financial benefits of reduced transaction costs.

Summary

The architecture of the construction industry is at a cross-roads. Will firms become involved in intronets based on dependency relationships or supranets based on consortia? Whatever path is taken, organizations should be mindful of the sustainable advantage that it offers. Will it simply end up in a zero-sum game whereby the only beneficiary is the client – where the operational efficiency boundary is pushed forward with no increase in profits? An understanding of fit will be important in identifying the sustainable aspect of these decisions. For firms that are able to see and respond to this upheaval the opportunities are great.

KEY POINTS FROM THIS CHAPTER

- E-commerce is more than electronic data interchange.

- Agent technology offers considerable possibilities for optimizing the buying and selling process.

- Construction firms should identify an e-commerce framework.

- An e-commerce framework establishes the types of e-commerce relationships that are sought and the location of the trading partners relative to the firewall.

- Two types of extranet enable trading with external partners – the intronet and the supronet. The choice of approach has particular strategic significance.

8

Creating an Internet architecture

Questions addressed in this chapter

- Is simply sharing electronic information on the Internet enough?

- What obstacles to interoperability still exist and how can they be overcome?

- Is there a common electronic language that will enable firms within the construction industry to interoperate over the Internet?

- What are the characteristics of this common exchange language?

- How do I create and deliver information over the Internet using this common exchange language?

- Why should an Internet-based construction industry replace 'documents' with 'information components'?

- What are the benefits of jumping from a simple electronic copy of the paper-based model to a process model designed specifically to make use of the e-commerce environment?

What is the problem?

So you have created a web site of your construction firm providing in-depth information about your services. You may have created an intranet system that allows departments around the world to exchange files and project data. But does that make your firm Internet ready for the future? The answer probably is 'no' – many of the problems that existed prior to networking capabilities still exist. The Internet has not solved these problems and may indeed have made the problems more conspicuous. Let us consider some of these:

- Information created and stored by specific software applications cannot be brought into other software applications. The construction industry uses a plethora of different types and makes of software application. Software applications include planning and scheduling, cost modelling, computer aided design, engineering design and many others. Considerable time and effort are spent entering information into these systems and the outputs that they produce are often only capable of being reused within the software environment they were created in.
- Information is created by a variety of different firms on a construction project, each using their own proprietary solutions and operating systems.
- Information is created at many different stages in the construction lifecycle. Without the tools to transfer information between packages used at different stages, much of the information is either lost or recreated at great expense.
- For project data that is available on line there is still no effective way of searching these documents in a sensible way. The potential of the computer environment to screen and filter information is lost because no consistent method is used to structure information in a way that can be understood by machines.

What are the options?

There have been many false dawns in the construction industry with respect to IT. The arrival of new standards and software solutions has promised seamless integration between software applications and companies, but the reality has been very different. What kinds of integration models have been proposed and why have they consistently failed? Let us look at a few of them in turn.

Neutral file formats

Many intranet and extranet systems currently being used in construction projects use conventional file exchange to transfer information between software applications. Because of the diversity of file formats, many software applications have been developed to allow the reading and writing of information in a variety of file formats. Neutral file formats have also been developed that are vendor independent and allow a variety of software applications to exchange information. For text transfer a common file format is rich text format (RTF), and for CAD drawings data exchange file (DXF) is a common neutral format. But there is an inherent conflict here.

Software developers are continually seeking to differentiate their own products from others on the market through 'feature enrichment'. Inevitably this creates information that can no longer be accommodated in a neutral format or in other vendors' formats. Every file exchange process with other applications results in a process of information loss – rather like the process of copying copies on a photocopy machine over several iterations, the returned file is often a poor reproduction of the original.

Application programming interfaces

A concept that has received interest among the computer programming fraternity since the late 1980s is that of 'application programming interfaces'. The idea here is that computer applications reveal some of their internal workings in the form of a hook, known as an API (application programming interface). Provided the user of one application knows the published APIs of another program, they are able to access and exchange data. Because this process relies on function calls rather than file exchanges the integrity of the data is superior to that from file exchanges. However, construction firms are still faced with the problem of employing experts in the various API protocols used by different applications, each of which is unique. Moreover, because of the tight definition of the protocols, new versions of applications can often cause exchange processes to cease working. In short, the construction industry cannot afford the investment in programming expertise required to make applications talk to one another in this way.

Project databases

Perhaps the most widely touted idea in construction in connection with interoperability is the idea of a project model – a repository where all information pertaining to a construction project is located and is accessible over the Internet. Applications are made to store their information on this database in a predefined manner that is accessible to all other applications. Across a project intranet or extranet the various firms involved in the project are able to maintain their part of the project model and control access from other participants. In practice, the idea of a super-database of project information has proved difficult to implement. Several fundamental problems arise from this approach including the performance penalty of applications writing to the database, the costs involved in reengineering software application to work with a common database, and the difficulties associated with structural changes to such a database.

Having considered the shortcomings of the above solutions it is perhaps no surprise that many construction firms have remained firmly encamped in the world of hardcopy, fax and email. But the time has come when construction firms can no

Table 8.1 Merits of different forms of construction information exchange over the Internet. (Key: *** = good)

Characteristic	File exchange	APIs	Project database	aecXML
Easily implemented	**		***	***
No lossy transfer		***	***	***
Requires no programming expertise	***			***
No performance penalty	***	***		***
Universal standard				***
Operates with outside industry standards	*			***
Extensible (can incorporate new features)				***
Requires no direct communication between applications	***			***

longer continue to rely on these outmoded forms of document exchange. An inevitable gap will begin to develop between those firms that use these technologies and do not buy into the emerging method of information exchange based on the extensible markup language (XML). Table 8.1 illustrates the merits of standard markup language for the architectural, engineering and construction industries (aecXML) compared to the other three methods of information exchange.

What is aecXML?

Earlier on we looked at the characteristics of XML. We noted that it is from the same family of languages as hypertext markup language (HTML) – the language responsible for the success of the Internet. Indeed it is the very simplicity of the HTML language – that is nothing more than a collection of special keywords or tags – that has made it such a successful language. It can be authored with rudimentary software tools and, unlike application documents such as word-processor files, the coding is transparent and nonproprietary. However, we also noted earlier that in many ways the Internet has outgrown HTML, particularly in relation to commercial applications. Industries are looking for much more control and less unambiguity in their documents. The tremendous flexibility in producing Web pages authored in HTML is also one of its limitations.

As the name suggests, extensible markup language (XML) enables information exchange to use extensible tags rather than a limited number of tags concerned with the presentation of text (as is the case with HTML). Many industries are now busily developing their own XML tags that will enable powerful information exchange based on agreed industry standards. The architecture and construction industry is no exception. As recently as September 1999 the first working draft of the aecXML specification was published over the Internet. This was produced by a consortium of software vendors, contractors and academics involved in the construction industry.

The aecXML schema was conceived as a framework for using the XML standard for electronic communications in the architectural, engineering and construction industries.

So, what kinds of information exchange will aecXML enable over the Internet? Consider the various users and applications that might be using it in the construction industry.

Scenario 1 – specifying

An architect is designing a leisure facility and needs to search for rooflights with the following properties:

- glass fibre splayed
- size approximately 1200 × 900
- dome shaped
- acrylic glazing
- double-skin insulation
- light transmission greater than 85%
- high impact strength.

Scenario 2 – quality assurance

An architect then wishes to check the quality assurance standard of the items identified:

- BS2782: 1970 Method 508A conformant – burning characteristics – slow burning
- BS2782: Part 7: 1987 – Surface spread of flame – Class 3
- BS476: Part 3: 1975 External Fire Exposure Roof Test – DDX.

Scenario 3 – availability

A contractor wants to find out about the availability of the roof-light product identified by the architect and the availability of similar products.

Scenario 4 – integration

A design tool is to be integrated with a cost modelling program.

Scenario 5 – expertise

A client wishes to identify what contractors have done work on hospital facilities in the South-West of Australia with construction costs greater than $12 million.

Scenario 6 – supply

A lighting manufacturer wishes to identify the types of lighting units required in a design document and match this with their available product line.

Scenario 7 – e-commerce

A contractor would like to pull out quantities from an estimating tool and send a procurement request to suppliers over the Internet.

The range of examples above indicates the breadth of possibilities currently being addressed using the aecXML schema. Some of the examples above involve the use of complex search mechanisms (and therefore structured source documents). Others make use of real-time information, as in Scenario 3 where real-time information on availability can be accessed. Others make use of strict exchange rules as in the e-commerce example in Scenario 7. Yet other examples illustrate how aecXML can be used to enable machine-to-machine integration, as in Scenario 4.

Types of information encompassed in aecXML

The types of information used in architecture and construction and addressed in the aecXML schema include those discussed below.

Documents

Many types of document used in construction have a semistructured format making them ideal candidates for XML markup. These include requests for information (RFI), requests for quotes, drawing specifications, addenda, change orders, contracts, building codes and purchase orders.

Building components

As well as items identifiable from catalogues, many building components are described in terms of customized parameters. Components may take the form of complex assemblies that can also be defined. Bulk materials may be described and defined in terms of composition and material properties.

Projects

Projects can be identified using unique identifiers and characterized in terms of start and finish dates, location, lifecycle stages (design, construction, decommissioning).

Professional services and resources

Provides a systematic way of describing professional services using XML including engineers, architects, contractors, suppliers and specialities.

Organizations

Information relating to standards bodies, research establishments and government agencies.

Software

Information characterizing software applications in construction identifying their principal use (CAD, estimating, document management) and including various other characteristics of interest to enable exchange of information.

AecXML schema and emerging XML capabilities

One of the confusing points for people trying to understand Internet concepts is that the Internet itself is undergoing continual evolution. Even during its brief existence, XML is undergoing some fairly fundamental changes. Some of these changes will greatly increase its potential, but for the newcomer these changes can seem disconcerting. Four concepts are worth knowing about and are the subject of new recommendations by the World Wide Web Consortium.

Schema

In computer programming a schema is the organization or structure of a database. In XML a schema is a model for describing the structure of information. The aecXML schema thus embodies all of the structural elements required to represent a whole class of information types used in construction (documents, projects, organizations, software and so forth). The schema describes the types of tags that can be used, their arrangement and their attributes (for example, 'draft' might be the status attribute of a contract document). Essentially a schema defines the ground-rules of a document, ensuring that a common vocabulary is used when exchanging documents. The process of checking whether XML documents conform to these rules is known as validation.

Schemas are designed to replace document type definitions (DTDs). The DTD historically is the method for representing document structure in the SGML family of languages (of which XML is one). XML schemas represent a dramatic departure from DTDs, breaking the link with SGML in an attempt to overcome some of the shortcomings of XML. Some of the limitations of DTDs include:

- They are created using a different syntax to the XML documents themselves.
- They do not support namespaces (see below).
- The options for controlling data types are extremely limited. For example, if we wanted to apply information about a project, i.e. <project>, regarding project start time, the looseness of a DTD definition would allow the author to enter almost any text string. There are no facilities for describing numbers, dates and currency values.
- It is difficult within a DTD to make relationships explicit between elements.

XML schemas are much more expressive than DTDs and this will greatly increase the commercial scope of the XML language. In schemas, models are described in terms of *constraints*. A constraint defines what can appear in any given context. There are two kinds of constraint: content model constraints that describe the order and sequence of elements, and data type constraints that describe valid units of data.

Thus for example, the content model might constrain the appearance of information on a project's start date using the <begindate> element. This would only be allowed to occur once within a <project> tag and would have to take a data type of type date.

Namespace

Without clear definitions, XML is vulnerable to misinterpretation by authors and users of information. Simply tagging data elements is not enough. Users must share an understanding of what the tagging element represents, as the following situation illustrates. If I use

<contractor > Bloggs Lifting Equipment</contractor>

And another individual uses

<company>Bloggs Lifting Equipment </company>

we may have used different tags to imply the same meaning. How do we know we mean the same thing? Potentially more problematic are situations where the same tag is used for different purposes. For example <title> might be used by one author to indicate the identity of a project, while the same tag might be used by another author to indicate a document name. To overcome this difficulty, each tag or element needs to be linked to an unambiguous definition. This is achieved by declaring at the beginning of an XML document the location where the meaning of each data element or attribute is to be found. The namespace is an on-line file that defines the data element. The author simply has to enter the Web location of the schema in question (in this case aecXML). For aecXML this would be:

- `xmlns = ''urn:schema-microsoft-com:xml-data''`
- `xmlns:dt = ''urn:schemas-microsoft-com:xml-datatypes''`

where the first line defines the location of the data element definitions and the second line indicates the location of the data types.

Having a single place to describe the elements for a particular XML definition achieves three things:

- it removes the need to send the information along with each XML file;
- it allows many XML files to share a common namespace definition with its set of element definitions;
- it enables the addition of further elements to the namespace over time.

XPath and XPointer

Currently, navigation between information on the Web is not very sophisticated. You can jump from one Web page to another but you cannot pinpoint where precisely in a given Web page you might want to go. Part of the problem is that Web-based information has no logical structure. The XPath proposed recommendation by the World Wide Web Consortium seeks to create common syntax and semantics for querying the contents of XML documents. XPath derives it name from its use of 'path' notation as is used in Web addresses (URLs or uniform resource locators). It operates on an abstract level, seeing documents as a tree of nodes. XPointer is a development of XPath. It allows the traversal of a document tree and choice of its internal parts based on various properties, such as element types, attribute values, character content and relative position.

Being an XML schema, the possibilities for e-commerce offered by aecXML are profound. It will be able to exploit the fruits of many developments in XML standards so that it becomes the obvious method of information exchange in the construction industry. Because the aecXML standard is based on simple element definitions, there is plenty of room for the creation of new element definitions. XLinks and XPointers will allow complex interaction between information elements like project data, scheduling information and project specifications. The more rigorous methods for controlling data types will enable more reliable exchange of data between computer systems. This will be particularly useful in the area of electronic data exchange that has so far been hampered by the lack of control over data types.

However, considerable delay and controversy continue to affect the implementation of these new XML innovations. XML schemas were supposed to be a proposed recommendation by December 1999, but at the time of writing were still in the form of a working draft. (Unlike standards bodies, the World Wide Web Consortium does not release standards but recommendations. A recommendation is the final stage of formalizing the guidelines of the World Wide Web Consortium.) However, firms involved in the construction industry need to be putting systems in place now, in time for the imminent arrival of these recommendations.

Elements in the aecXML specification

The preliminary specification for the aecXML schema encompasses a large number of tags to enable rich transfer of information for the types of document discussed above. Table 8.2 provides a flavour of how the framework is being developed. As the schema develops, the hierarchical levels will increase, allowing greater precision in marking up information.

The aecXML schema is being developed along the lines of other industry schemas. Some of the important characteristics of the schema are as follows:

- It is designed with simplicity in mind, allowing design and construction firms of varying levels of IT sophistication to make use of the technology.
- It is not designed as a classification system. Several suitable classification systems for building components already exist. The schema is designed to provide sufficient flexibility to allow alternative classifications.
- Several other XML schemas are emerging that are applicable to all industries. The aecXML schema does not reproduce these but will be sufficiently open to allow the inclusion of other schemas. Examples include industry schemas for purchase orders, e-commerce, STEP and various other financial and engineering schemas.
- Considerable interest is developing around a schema that supports standard queries for XML information. XML-QL (XML query language) and XQL (extensible query language) are among the competing proposals. The aecXML schema should be capable of leveraging the considerable power of these refined query systems.

The XML schema concept has acquired considerable momentum in all industries keen to see the wholesale implementation of e-commerce; however, a word of caution is appropriate here. At the time of writing, there were no commercial editors for creation of XML schemas. There continues to be debate about the merits of the

Table 8.2 An illustration of elements (tags) use in the aecXML schema.

Element name	Description	Some elements contained in the element
\<aecxml\>	This is the outermost element in the aecXML schema. The element includes information on namespaces (i.e. definitions regarding the elements contained in it) as well as version information.	All aecXML elements are contained by this element.
\<document\>	This element is used to represent a plethora of document types including drawings, specifications, purchase orders and safety data. The hierarchical arrangement of elements contained in this should enable intuitive navigation of various types of document. The use of XPointer and XPath will be an important facility in this respect.	\<DocumentSet\> \<DocumentState\> \<DocumentType\>
\<BuildingComponent\>	One of the key elements in the schema, the building component element is being formulated to reflect all lifecycle stages. A distinction is made between discrete products, items that involve customization (e.g. lifts), assemblies and bulk materials.	\<DiscreteItem\> \<CustomItem\> \<Assembly\> \<Material\>
\<DiscreteItem\>	This element description is used for construction products that can be purchased by selection from a catalogue (in contrast to custom items, assemblies and materials – see above). Associated with this element would be a classification, a set of performance characteristics (allowing comparison between products) and an Internet address (URL).	\<DesignData\> \<EstimationData\> \<ScheduleData\> \<MaintenanceData\> \<DesignationData\>
\<Classification\>	The purpose of the aecXML schema is not to produce an exhaustive classification system. It is sufficiently open to allow the use of a number of established classification systems. For example: `<Classification domain=''MasterFormat'', value =''07240''></Classification>`	
\<Request\> \<Response\>	This combination of elements allows two-way communication between software applications. The use of globally unique identifiers with these elements will enable sophisticated search mechanisms.	

XML schema approach and the extent to which it improves on the DTD approach used in the existing XML environment. As well as a widespread support for tools to create XML using DTDs (including Framemaker plus SGML™ by Adobe and XMetal™ by Softquad) a large number of document types are already defined using DTDs in various industries.

The discussion so far has shown how the construction industry itself is beginning to define its own language as part of the Internet – through the adoption of aecXML. The industry is also recognizing areas of commonality with other industries that share similar procedures and document types. Astute firms will make use of markup standards for information exchange beyond traditional industry boundaries. Such firms will benefit from the considerable effort being invested in these exchange standards, particularly in the area of electronic data interchange.

Demise of the document

One of the dearly beloved objects of the construction industry is the 'document'. This love affair has persisted during its translation to the electronic form. The book entitled the *Digital Document* (Duyshart, 1997) describes the evolution of the digital document in architecture and construction. Whether it be tender bids, contracts or requests for information, the document as an entity has managed to retain its identity. But the sacrosanct nature of the document is now being challenged. This is because of the possibilities of advanced publishing applications. These include personalized Web pages, push-model Web publishing, modular documentation and customer information services. Increasingly, these forms of communication rely, not on the document, but on components of information and collections of components.

Many firms in construction would argue that information management in their organization is highly efficient, using standard forms and a formalized processing sequence. However, unlike the construction site, where inefficiencies are made readily apparent, inefficiencies in information management are all too invisible. Some common causes of the information gap are:

* Information is delayed in the design process until a point is reached when a complete document is satisfactorily dealt with by one individual or organization. Only when the document is completed in its entirety can it be signed off and passed on in the design process.
* Co-authoring of documents is not possible as there is no reliable way of tracking changes and identifying the originating organization or individual.
* Information is invariably in the wrong form to be used for another purpose.
* Information may need to be assembled from a number of different sources.
* Information is typically hidden within documents containing other irrelevant information.
* Information is often unavailable, particularly when it is owned by different contractors on the project.
* Information is out of date because of the difficulties of maintaining it.

So, despite the wonders of electronic exchange, we are still obligated by the checks and constraints that existed when paper-based systems were in use.

During the 1990s, construction firms invested substantial amounts in document management systems. Some of these are bespoke systems, others are off-the-shelf packages. Many of them have attempted to address some of the shortcomings identified above – sophisticated methods for recording the status of drawings, the version history of tender documents or the identity of authors. More contemporary systems are now Internet enabled, allowing users to exchange files and author documents. However, most of the systems still require a sequential process of authoring and retain the document as the definitive level of transport. The following sections explore an approach that transforms the process of information management and frees up information from the document.

From paperless to documentless

Many of the causes of the information gap described previously, arise from the compartmentalization of information into documents. For many information applications in construction, the document is vital in terms of providing context for the information. For example, information contained in a contract only has legal significance in relation to the document as a whole. However, many types of information can be used independently. For example, a paragraph from one tender document might be required in another part of a tender submission. An instructional procedure in a health-and-safety manual might also be incorporated into part of a company's on-line safety manual (perhaps in a slightly different format). The temptation might be to copy-and-paste such information but this kind of practice is a common cause of error. When the original item is updated, the copied item remains in the original form (providing out of date information) or will require additional work in terms of identifying and editing. This process of duplicate information springing up and evolving down independent paths produces major costs for construction firms. By failing to make good use of available information through reuse and the effects of working on out-of-date information (often the cause of rework) construction firms are exposing themselves to significant costs.

So what is the solution? Does Web technology really enable us to work in a documentless as well as a paperless office? The following section describes in detail an approach being used by major manufacturers (including car manufacturers) to achieve document delivery. The approach is based on the use of existing XML technology and is yielding major savings by bridging the information gap. This approach involves the use of a number of key concepts implemented using an authoring and publishing environment enabled through the Web.

Components and collections

A component of information describes any piece of information that can be used independently. For example, the version number of a drawing is a component and might be contained in a CAD drawing, but made available for other documents such as a request for information or a work audit. Other components might include instructional procedures, an order quantity, a catalogue number or parts of a detailed brief.

Although these components of information might be useful on their own, more often than not a collection of components is required to express a complete thought or to resolve a problem. Such collections are assemblies of components put together for a specific purpose. A collection might be marketing material put together for a specific client or an installation guide for a particular subcontractor.

Invariably, collections of information need to be used for various types of media, making it necessary to separate the issues of media-specific formatting from content. Furthermore, the content may need to be adjusted to suit the particular type of media. For example, Web content requires bite-size chunks of screen information and low-resolution images, whereas printed documents make use of larger items of information and high-resolution images. To avoid complete reworking for each media type a system of tailored reuse is essential. The key concepts underlying the component model are:

- *Component capture* – In order to make information usable at the very granular level of components, a company-wide system must be in place to enable components to be identified and characterized. By creating documents in an XML environment sufficient control can be imposed on the data types to ensure that information is meaningful to computer applications and humans. Various tools can also be used to obtain component information from legacy documents (e.g. Microsoft Word documents).

- *Component context management* – The context of information is as important as the content itself. This means that a structuring system and linking system must be in place to enable components to be used in multiple contexts.

- *Component reuse* – The process of reusing data from a single source helps to ensure that information is consistent. The reuse of information not only reduces unnecessary authoring but more importantly ensures that information is up to date even when it is used in a separate context.

- *Component control* – An increasing number of document management systems used in the construction industry allow control in a co-authoring environment. This is achieved by security, access controls and by check-in and check-out facilities (whereby a document is made unavailable to others during the time that one individual is working on it). However, using the more granular component level rather than the document level of control, considerably more flexibility is enabled. Individual elements and collections can be worked on by one individual or organization while allowing other elements and collections within the same document to be authored by another party. This finer level of authoring control can substantially reduce the time required to produce information (such as a tender document), because the whole document does not have to be locked up by one individual or organization.

- *Component auditing* – A document history enables information managers to develop an audit trail of who has done what to a document. This may be of interest for a number of reasons:

  - The design manager may wish to establish who has looked at the document as part of the authorization process.
  - The architect or builder may need to identify who made particular changes in the event of design errors.
  - A project manager may wish to identify the time spent on a particular activity and possibly evaluate the personnel time committed by different organizations.

The advantage of having a document history at the component level rather than the document level is that a much more detailed history is available. It becomes possible to examine the history of specific components, identifying what changes were made, by whom and over what period of time.

Designing an XML-based information management system

A number of emerging solutions enable information management at the component level. All of these exploit the benefits of XML for identifying components or elements. The following description provides an illustration of one system architecture. However, there are a number of system architectures that could be used to achieve the same outcome (albeit with varying performance).

The system architecture shown in Figure 8.1 contains the essential components of an information system for semistructured data delivered using XML. This involves the following:

- an authoring environment to enable individuals to access and amend content on the XML database;
- a system for publishing and accessing XML files generated from the database.

Such a system could be used for any sizeable data store involving semistructured data. Information content might include structured contract documents, tender documents, project information, specifications and many other types of information.

Table 8.3 shows some of the commercial applications and interface languages that can be used in an XML Internet architecture similar to Figure 8.1.

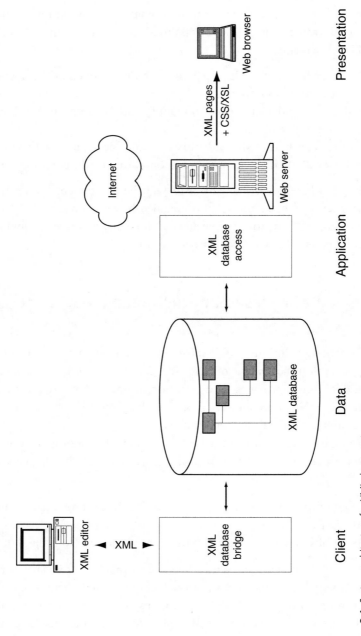

Fig. 8.1 System architecture for XML document management.

Table 8.3 Applications required for an XML database system.

System part	Stage	Purpose	Interfaces	Commercial products
XML editor	Content creation	Used to create XML content. Uses check-in and check-out facility to enable co-authoring.	XML database bridge provides access to the database.	XMetal (Softquad) Framemaker + SGML
XML database	Content repository	Contains XML documents broken down into components. Document structure represented as a tree structure with cross-links.	Enables controlled access to XML editor and interacts with Web server using C++ and API calls.	Astoria (Chrystal) POET Software
Web server	Content publishing	Provides XML data as well as Internet programs to enable interactive queries.	May make use of Java technology (servlets or applets).	Jigsaw (W3C)
Web Browser		Provides user access to the information presented as XML files.	XML files may be processed on the Web server side or by the browser.	Internet Explorer 5+ (Fifth-generation browsers)

Content creation

Several editor software applications are now available to enable authors to create XML documents. The creation of XML documents should not be confused with the development of the document type definitions (DTDs). Once a document type has been defined, the process of marking up information is no more complicated than writing word processor documents. The authors may be secretarial support or managers within firms writing their own material. The editors enable the user to mark up information using a library of tags defined in the DTDs. They also check to see whether the XML documents are:

- well formed – in essence they have a structure that conforms to the general require-ments of an XML page,
- valid – that is, they conform to the specific constraints imposed by the particular DTD it is associated with.

Two common XML editors are Framemaker + SGML (shown in Figure 8.2) and XMetal (shown in Figure 8.3). The screenshot of XMetal also shows an additional menu bar that allows the user to access much of the functionality of the XML database Astoria^{TM}. The information author can browse the database, look at component histories, examine structure and reuse components.

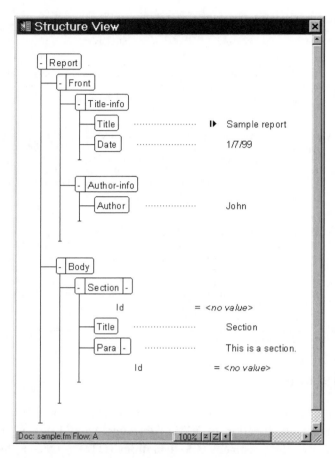

Fig. 8.2 Using the XML editor Framemaker + SGML to create content.

BladeRunner™ by Interleaf uses a menu-system add-on within Word™ to enable Word™ to function as an XML editor. Facilities include save, view, validate and email. This enables users to make use of a common word-processing environment to generate XML. The author creates a standard Word or Interleaf document using the Word template, is guided through the structure of the XML DTD and is given lists of choices for valid content. BladeRunner then validates the document against the DTD and generates XML from within the authoring environment.

Content repository

The XML database stores information in the form of a tree structure, similar to files on a computer. Figure 8.4 shows how documents are stored within the database. Also

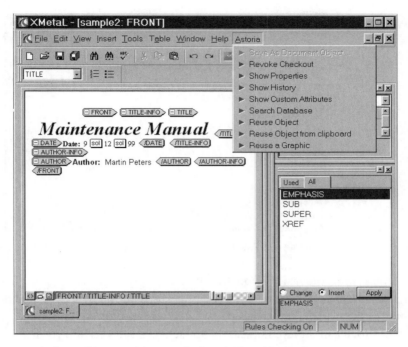

Fig. 8.3 XMetal editor making use of the XML database bridge with Astoria.

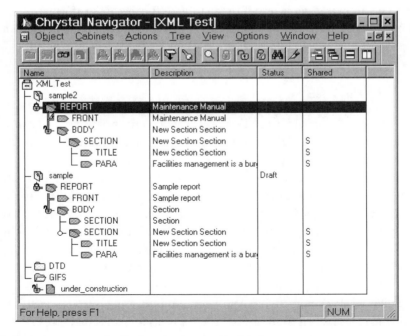

Fig. 8.4 Context management – the tree structure used in Astoria.

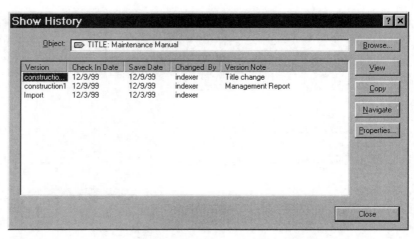

Fig. 8.5 History of an XML document in Astoria showing a change in content for the Title component.

notice the use of padlock icons on the directory tree to show what components are currently checked out. Reused data can be used in these tree structures using cross-links to the original information.

The repository can store complete component histories as shown in Figure 8.5 using Astoria. This includes not only a description of the changes but previous content as well. At first sight the idea of storing complete version histories may appear to be an extravagant use of data storage. But because information is stored at the component level, changes produce copies of the component itself, not the whole document.

Content publishing

The final process of publishing can be achieved in a number of ways. The appeal of an XML database is the flexibility afforded to create many different forms of output from the same source.

The new generation of browser technology (version 5 and above for Internet Explorer and Netscape) is capable of interpreting XML files sent over the Internet. This is achieved by a parser within the browsers that is capable of checking XML files for validity according to a DTD associated with the page. A short-term issue relates to the widespread use of earlier browser technologies that are not capable of viewing XML files. For this reason, some system architectures choose to create HTML at the server side. This enables users with earlier browsers to view XML content with a similar level of interactivity. Another reason for using this approach is that the underlying DTD is hidden from the user. For reasons of intellectual property or security many construction firms might prefer to hide this aspect of their information system.

KEY POINTS FROM THIS CHAPTER

This chapter has described the possibilities of information management that sheds the constraints of the traditional document. Some of the key issues addressed include:

- The problems associated with many established and emerging forms of information exchange.

- The possibilities offered by an industry standard markup language (aecXML) and some of the difficulties that remain to be resolved.

- The extent and impact of the information gap in the construction process.

- The reasons why the use of *components of information* can overcome this information gap.

- The type of system architecture that will enable components of information to be used, reused and tracked.

9

Creating an Internet system specification

Questions addressed in this chapter

- How does my firm go about planning an Internet system?

- Why use a planned approach to the adoption of Internet systems in construction firms?

- What do we mean by an enterprise Internet architecture?

- What steps are involved in creating an Internet system?

- How do I describe where my IT system is now?

- How do I define where we should be in terms of a target architecture?

- What are the potential pitfalls?

Importance of planning

So, you are about to develop your own system using Internet technology in the form of an intranet, extranet or globally accessible Internet site. Having considered all of the developments in Internet technology discussed in previous chapters, you might well feel daunted by the prospect of embarking on such an undertaking. Just knowing the technological opportunities is not enough. Managers can quickly be drawn into producing solutions looking for problems. You may have already undertaken an Internet project with some success, without the need for a formal planning process. But undefined processes provide only short-term fixes. How do you ensure that you get consistent results? How do you monitor progress? A formal process involving a number of well-defined steps will provide a strong basis for delivering tangible business benefits from a project.

From fire-fighting to long-term planning

One of the problems faced by firms involved in the construction process is that IT systems often form part of a one-off construction project. For example, an extranet system might be funded to enable the exchange of drawings on a project between the main contractor and subcontractors. Each subcontractor is persuaded to buy-into a technological solution with the enticement of hardware and software. The main contractor derives benefit from reduced transaction costs but the subcontractors have to train personnel and acquire expertise all within the space of a few weeks at the outset of the project. The main contractor may have to create an information system unique to a project because it has to satisfy the idiosyncrasies of the client requirements. Moreover, because of the high-pressure time constraints that the successful contractor has to operate in, having won a project, the information system is then designed as a quick fix. Issues of reusability, modularity and interoperability are sacrificed. The net result is that subcontractors are on a continual merry-go-round stepping from one information system to another. Hardware and software become obsolete and staff have to be retrained in different systems. Information systems differ not just from one contractor to another but from one project to another.

To some extent the use of Internet technology will reduce such problems – but will certainly not eliminate them. The use of a standard application (the Web browser) and an open exchange protocol (TCP/IP) removes many of the obstacles previously encountered. But even Internet technologies provide infinite opportunity for reinvention! User interfaces can be changed, underlying processes can be modified and business functions evolve. Against this uncertain backdrop, a formal planning process that extends beyond single projects becomes critical for firms seeking to leverage benefit from Internet projects.

Enterprise architecture

What do we mean by an 'enterprise' and by an 'enterprise architecture'? The term 'enterprise' is increasingly used to refer to a chain of firms involved in the delivery process, often involving suppliers and customers. However, for the purpose of this chapter we think of the enterprise as any entity that has a common business purpose and a set of goals to meet it. So we can think of a buying department as an enterprise or a chain of geographically dispersed organizations as an enterprise.

An enterprise will often cut across functional groupings, departments and organizations. The purpose of the 'enterprise architecture' is to enable the enterprise to function across particular slices of the organizations involved. The flexible nature of Internet technologies has been particularly important in realizing the possibilities of enterprise architectures.

An enterprise architecture is not an information system but rather the big picture that defines how the entire organization works together. It may comprise one or many information systems and many groups of people, data, integration levels and subsystems.

Stages involved

Any Internet project of any size requires a structured planning process. Even if the construction or design firm involved is choosing to outsource the project, they will

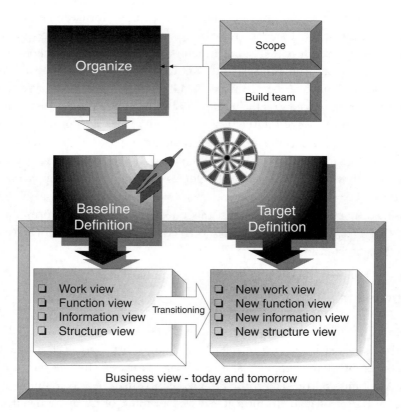

Fig. 9.1 Stages in Internet specification.

need to be heavily involved with the specification, monitoring and evaluation. Too many construction firms pay over the odds for the delivery of information systems (often because it involves a technology about which they are not knowledgeable and for which they are unable to establish a market price). Formal planning does not mean getting involved in a never-ending cycle of analysis. Such analysis-paralysis can be avoided by knowing how to scope the project effectively.

The three major steps involved in system planning are (Figure 9.1):

- *organizing* – whereby the extent of the project is outlined and the team members identified;
- *baseline definition* – achieved by an analysis of a firm's current baseline provision in terms of work, function, information and infrastructure;
- *target definition* – that describes the desired characteristics of the proposed Internet system.

These three stages lead to the creation of what Armour *et al.* (1999) call the 'target definition' (analogous to the brief or programme – the term 'programme' is used as the US counterpart to the more commonly used word 'brief' in the UK). Notice that most of the expertise revolves around strategic business issues rather than detailed technical ones.

Stage 1: Organizing

Without the right team and the right commitment from senior personnel in a firm, an Internet system is likely to fail. Organizing means identifying a feasible Internet project and the people required to make it happen. Key Internet projects may well have been flagged up by previous business process reengineering (BPR) or IT plans within a firm.

Scoping the project

The creation the target Internet architecture definition should ideally take no more than 6–8 months. Having a clear view of the proposed e-commerce business model is helpful at this stage – if only to clarify the particular nature of the system. Table 9.1 indicates possible types of business model. It is unlikely that the enterprise architecture is likely to span more than one of these business models. The cause of failure of many Internet projects stems from over-scoping. Internet projects seeking to 'Internet enable' all business processes are likely to fail because of unconstrained scope.

Table 9.1 Forms of e-commerce model (adapted from Lam, 1999).

E-commerce business model	Variations	Description	Internet technologies
Advertising		Using the Internet to advertise products or services	On-line database technology for up-to-date pricing
Marketing	Mailing lists and discussion boards		
	Market information gathering/client profiling using agent technology	Gathering and processing information about clients and customers	
Order processing	Order capture	Capturing orders for products and services over the Internet	
	Payment processing	Processing order payment	
	Stock control	Linking order capture to stock control	
	On-line tracking	Tracking orders for customer viewing	
Publishing	Company information dissemination		Web publishing (e.g. PDF)
	Project information dissemination		On-line document management
Collaborative working	CAD and 3D design		Object modelling
	Document co-authoring		XML database technology

Building the team

The team involved in the target Internet architecture definition typically should involve four to six people making up a core team, lead by the principal designer. Part of the principal designer's job is to evangelize the concept underlying the project. Functional experts (for example, logistics or contract administration) should be involved on a part-time basis providing expertise on a specific domain. Small projects or those involving more mature domains may require less resourcing from functional experts.

Establishing a target vision

Teams can soon become dysfunctional when understanding goes awry. One of the common causes is that key players are not included. One feature of enterprise architectures is that ill-informed decisions early on can have a profound effect. Engaging good consultants to offer advice and train team members is money well spent. The resulting enterprise architecture is much more likely to satisfy an organization's

Table 9.2 Stakeholders involved in an Internet project steering committee (based on Armour *et al.* (1999)).

Stakeholders	Their interest in the development process	Their priorities for the system
Customers or clients	As the financer of the project, the client will be concerned with project risk and the benefits to the enterprise.	Risk, budget, feasibility, acceptance criteria
Users	Users will be concerned to see that it meets their needs. They provide help in validating system performance.	Performance, reliability, interoperability, ease-of-use, accessibility
System architects	Translating requirements into an architectural definition for the project, the system architect will be involved in technology selection and performance standards.	Consistency, completeness, effectiveness
System developers	Using the architectural definition provided by the system architect, the system developer must implement a detailed solution with reference to the architect.	Technical feasibility, economy
System maintainers	Maintainers of the Internet system must be capable of evolving the solution in response to technological changes and changing functional requirements.	Reusability, transparency, modularity

mission. The shared target vision should extend beyond the core team: participation and dissemination of ideas is important. A frequent approach to ensure that people buy into the aims of the project is to set up an architecture steering committee comprising senior managers and functional experts. In formulating a vision Armour *et al.* (1999) suggest asking six questions:

1. Who are the stakeholders? Consider the different types of people likely to be affected by the system, including not only users but people who have to maintain and operate the system (Table 9.2).
2. What are the key issues or problems that exist at the enterprise level?
3. What is the relative significance of each of these problems?
4. How will important concepts be communicated?
5. What tools will be used?
6. Where will the team work?

Stage 2: Baseline views

This stage, frequently omitted from IT planning, seeks to establish where you are now. It is an essential step that will enable the planning team to gauge the difficulties of reaching their target system architecture. Many firms involved in construction do not have a high-level view of their IT usage and how this relates to business objectives.

If we are looking at enterprises involving a number of firms the knowledge of existing systems and scope for rationalizing may be even less clear.

The baseline definition stage is essentially concerned with creating an inventory of information systems within the enterprise, together with their various components and an understanding of the relationships between them. It will allow the planning team to establish 'who is using what and why?'. The process of creating an inventory of the existing enterprise system will help to isolate (a) the assets that are available, (b) the gaps that exist, and (c) the redundancies that exist. Armour *et al.* (1999) suggest developing four views of the enterprise:

- the work view
- the function view
- the information view
- the infrastructure view.

By analysing these in turn the planning team will be able to reveal a high-level view of the baseline system. Having created this picture the project team can then assess the difficulties involved in reaching the target vision. It also enables the team to gauge progress when transitioning from the baseline to the target system.

Work view

What are the processes involved in carrying out the activities of the enterprise? We might, for example, be considering an enterprise that has evolved as a coherent supply chain to produce curtain walling. A number of specialists including a sealant manufacturer, glass manufacturer, frame assembler, architectural detailer and a testing facility may all have developed as a recurring supply-chain sequence. When creating the work view a number of questions need to be answered (Figure 9.2):

- What are the products and services created by this enterprise?
- Who are the customers for the products and services?
- Who are the suppliers or providers of the products and services?
- Who are the specific organizational units within the respective firms that deal with the customers and supplier?
- What business functions and processes are used by the organizational units to enable them to work effectively?

This sequential process of questioning allows the project team to drill down from a general view of the enterprise to specific functional units within the organizations involved.

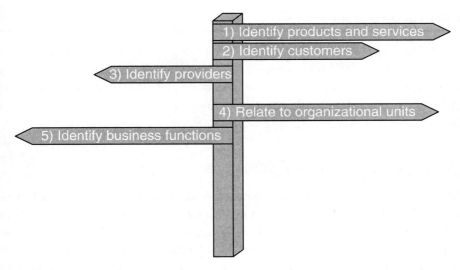

Fig. 9.2 Understanding the work view.

Function view

Having identified the various functions, the function view is concerned with characterizing the various IT applications that are used to automate the functions as well as
the information entities associated with them. This requires an understanding of the
dependencies between applications (for example, between a purchasing system used
by a contractor and an inventory system used by a lift supplier) as well as the
scope of the applications.

The people element is also important here. What is the distribution of people using
the applications? Are they working as teams? Are they co-located or geographically
dispersed? Are they mobile workers or office based?

Information view

This view provides an understanding of how the corporate data model fits
together and the relationships within it. Most processes and functions have a particular set of document types associated with them supported by some form of
data dictionary. Sequential processes will often have an evolutionary path of
document development associated with them (e.g. requests for information are
followed by a feedback document) that need to be mapped out. Techniques such as
data flow diagrams and structured analysis are useful for generating the information
view.

Infrastructure view

In order to produce a clear view of an enterprise's infrastructure, information on hardware, software and telecommunications technologies must be obtained. For Internet development, weaknesses in infrastructure may have implications for bandwidth, security and mobility of users in the target architecture.

Stage 3: Target definition

The final stage is not concerned with 'where you are' but with 'where you need to be'. This desired state is known as the target and the recipe for getting to it is known as the 'target definition'. The architecture of the envisaged Internet system is much more than an update of the existing baseline system characterized in the previous step. It constitutes a vision of the future. Although it may involve the use of legacy systems, it will also include significant enhancements possibly supporting new operations.

Business view

The target architecture must reflect a complex reality and will be developed by an iterative rather than a one-shot process. The starting point for the target definition is understanding the business needs. For example, the business focus may be on increasing customer interaction and tailored solutions. For the Internet architecture this will suggest more flexible design solutions, better client feedback and perhaps more innovative procurement methods. Another enterprise may be seeking to operate in a more heterogeneous environment involving many project partners. The onus is then on creating more interoperable systems and more integrated IT systems.

One popular method for expressing a project vision in terms of a business need is the balanced score-card (BSC) method. The four business perspectives used to evaluate a project are:

- *Financial* – This perspective reflects the interests of the shareholder and incorporates information on productivity, resource utilization, efficiency and investment opportunities.
- *Customer satisfaction* – This perspective is vital to long-term survival and makes use of information on customer satisfaction and retention, market share and profitability.
- *Business process effectiveness* – This perspective focuses on the opportunity for business improvements and scalability. Advances relating to improved document management, effective work processes and modes of operation are key areas.

- *Innovation and learning* – This perspective emphasizes the contribution of a new system to sustainable organizational growth through innovation and learning. Advances in an Internet-based enterprise architecture are likely to result in increased employee assets, information systems capabilities and technology competencies.

Target views

When looking at the baseline of the existing enterprise system the key views of work, function, information and infrastructure were considered. The target view considers each of these again in terms of a desired state.

Target work view

Do the emerging business needs demand new organizational units? Are processes aligned with the activities of the enterprise? Does Internet capability suggest more effective business groupings with customers and suppliers?

Target function view

Having identified the new objectives of the enterprise, does the target view encompass the various functions required to meet these objectives?

Target information view

The target architecture must include IT applications capable of providing the necessary information for the enterprise. Do the information standards currently in place need to be further evolved to fit with the new architecture?

Target infrastructure view

Does the new target architecture make existing systems obsolete? What systems should be modified, eliminated or decommissioned? What are the implications of multiple scenarios – for example, a 40% increase in Internet traffic?

By looking at each of these views in turn the project team should be able to make sense of what additional impacts a new enterprise architecture might have. The output from the target definition stage is the creation of a document that provides:

- an architectural overview of the desired enterprise system;
- a conceptual data model for the proposed system;

- a description of functional areas affected by the system (including any proposed process reengineering);
- a plan for executing the proposed target architecture.

Having defined the baseline system and a proposed target architecture, the Internet team should be well positioned to introduce Internet-enabled information systems within a construction firm. However, the process of creating a target architecture is a process – not an event. For this reason, it is necessary to continually review the business objectives and fine-tune the project accordingly.

KEY POINTS FROM THIS CHAPTER

- Not being an expert in Internet technology is no excuse for distancing yourself from the planning process.

- Understanding the business drivers is a key skill possessed by an in-house manager, and this skill needs to be exercised whether the project is undertaken in house or is outsourced.

- Planning an Internet project requires careful consideration of project scope. An Internet project seeking only to Internet-enable existing information systems is likely to be highly constrained and unfocused.

- Planning an Internet project is best considered at the enterprise level. The enterprise may cut through many parts of a business and through several stages of the value chain.

- The first stage of planning involves the creation of a sound and committed project team with the support of senior management and with all the key participants.

- The second stage of planning involves a structured analysis of the existing baseline system in terms of work, function, information and infrastructure.

- The final stage of planning involves a corresponding assessment of a proposed architecture based on a similar assessment of work, function, information and infrastructure.

Creating the future

Questions addressed in this chapter

- Should an Internet system be document driven or people driven?

- Should an Internet system rely on codification or personalization?

- How reusable is your information?

- What are the future trends in the construction industry?

- How prepared is your organization to tackle the future of the Internet?

The degree to which the reader, after finishing the book, finds himself thinking about, speculating about or trying to anticipate future events, will provide one measure of its effectiveness. (Toffler, 1970)

Introduction

Having looked at the various strands of the learning organization, we should now be in a position to ask ourselves 'where does this fit with my firm, with my profession and with my industry?' The picture portrayed in preceding chapters is of an Internet environment undergoing rapid change. So much so, that in a strategic sense, we may need to completely review our perception of the Internet. In only five years the World Wide Web went from being a simple repository of static documents to one of dynamic database driven documents. But it has not stopped there. In the next few years we can expect to see the displacement of information solely for human consumption by information both human-readable and machine-readable. Combined with this will be the arrival of agent technology that will allow autonomous knowledge working on the Internet. Even as we retire home from our day at the drawing office or the construction site, our agents will be busy picking up snippets of information, looking for changes and opportunities that would otherwise pass us by.

All good strategies require trade-offs. Indeed, good strategies are based on clarity about what you intend *not* to do as much as what you intend to do. An Internet strategy is no exception. So, what are the critical trade-offs for design and construction firms? We know that the Internet has liberated us from the time-honoured theory surrounding the economics of information. Today we can achieve both richness and reach. The chapter on visibility showed how encoding provided a way of achieving information richness. In a later chapter we saw how the power of Internet communities can also be used to increase both richness and reach. But evidence suggests that the two approaches cannot be pursued equally without undermining or diluting them both. In this chapter, we look at this dichotomy and the different Internet strategies that the two paths entail. We see how an Internet strategy is enmeshed with the idea of a knowledge management strategy.

Document driven or people driven?

Two of the case studies covered earlier in the book highlighted contrasting approaches to knowledge management. Bechtel, the international construction firm is an example of an organization in pursuit of the people-to-document approach. Using this strategy, information is extracted from people in the organization as a result of work on particular construction projects. Once this information is elicited, it is stored in an electronic repository. More importantly, it is capable of being used independently of the person that originated it. Information can be reused by many other people in many other projects. For an international organization like Bechtel, the benefit derived from knowledge reuse is considerable. Other Bechtel offices around the world are able to search for and retrieve information, be it information on clients, technologies, personnel or subcontractors.

The contrasting approach to knowledge management is apparent in the case study on Haenlein, the architectural practice. Its emphasis on person-to-person communication reflects the nature of the business. As a small practice, the benefits of scalability afforded by encoded knowledge are not there. Instead, the success of the business is dependent on the richness of the person-to-person interaction. Solutions are tailored to the specific needs of the client and it is this personalization that the client is paying for – the opportunities for information reuse are significantly less than for Bechtel.

This divergence in knowledge management strategy is apparent not only in the construction industry. Similar patterns are clear in the computer industry, the medical industry and the strategic consultancy business.

Take for example Ernst & Young, described by Hansen *et al.* (1999), an organization clearly undertaking a people-to-document strategy. As a consultancy firm they have invested heavily in a centre for business knowledge – a centre of 250 staff responsible for the codification process and maintenance of an electronic repository. This repository is filled with knowledge objects, i.e. discrete pieces of knowledge that have been created from past projects (after client-sensitive information has been removed). It is made available to staff throughout the world using a networked architecture. Employees in Ernst & Young are able to pull key information from this repository to use as marketing material, benchmark data, for work schedules or any other business use. One specific example is the Los Angeles office of Ernst & Young where individuals are able to rapidly acquire information about an unfamiliar manufacturing industry by accessing the organization's knowledge repository. From this, the office is able to identify other Ernst & Young material prepared by other offices around the world that have already worked on a similar project. The ready availability of client presentation material, previously developed solutions and cost analyses enables the office to rapidly tweak this information for their own needs. This has enabled a successful bid to be completed within 2 months instead of a typical 4–6 months. The project itself was able to save a total of one year because of the availability of programming documents, technical specifications and training materials. The process of extracting information from employees is vital to the success Ernst & Young's operation. People need to be encouraged to write down what they know and provide this in electronic form. At performance reviews, consultants are assessed on the basis of five key dimensions, one of which is their 'contribution to and knowledge of the knowledge asset of the firm' (cited by Hansen *et al.* (1999)).

The use of knowledge stores should not be confused with automation. The codification process empowers the individual to create something new by reconfiguring and reusing existing building blocks. The economic model behind this approach is based on the economics of reuse. In our richness versus reach model the emphasis is on the scalability of encoded knowledge allowing the information to reach a much larger audience. The reuse model is particularly effective for design or construction firms that are dealing with problems that recur over and over again. The value creation process through reuse enables clients to benefit from proven and robust solutions that have been fine tuned. Moreover, the service or product can be delivered at a more competitive price.

Many firms involved in construction have to deal with *tacit* knowledge rather than hard information. For these firms the personalization solution provides a more effective Internet strategy path. The architectural profession is an example of such an area, where richness prevails over reach and personal interaction is essential to arrive at a design solution. Typically, the problems facing such firms are difficult to systematize, and so reuse is not viable. Proximity and face-to-face contact is the established way of ensuring that this rich interaction is achieved. The key Internet path is that of creating customer communities (described in Chapter 5).

Document-based knowledge management is driven by technologies such as document management systems, databases, word processed documents, CAD drawings and, increasingly, by markup languages like XML, all of which were discussed in Chapter 3. However, for the personalization solution, Internet technologies are required that facilitate rather than carry out information transfer. These are the type of technologies described in the chapter on the creation of communities. In other words, technologies that either

- enable the identification of stakeholders and experts as a precursor to person-to-person communication (e.g. groupware and contact databases), perhaps in the form of an online community, or
- that closely resemble the person-to-person experience (using video conferencing or teleconferencing), providing a surrogate for real-life meetings.

Hansen *et al.* (1999) observed that the personalization strategy required only a modest investment in information technology. However, if a rich interaction such as video conferencing is to be used to mimic face-to-face interaction, it may in fact be the most demanding Internet strategy. High-bandwidth technologies are essential to achieve a virtual interaction of this kind. Table 10.1 shows how the dichotomy between personalization and codification creates a contrasting Internet strategy for the construction industry.

From a study of various US organizations Hansen *et al.* (1999) concluded that the successful implementers of knowledge management were those that chose not to try to be both codifiers and personalizers. From our model of the learning organization, this suggests that success is achieved by an Internet strategy that focuses either on creating visibility or on creating communities. Each of these approaches is considered in preceding chapters of this book, together with the type of technologies used to support them. Trying to straddle both of these approaches produces poor results. For example, organizations leveraging the Internet through codified solutions would undermine their strategic fit if they have to overinvest in person-to-person solutions. Unnecessary innovation, reinvention and tailored solutions compromise the value proposition concerning the reuse of information. However, for other businesses involved in the construction industry the codified approach is likely to lead to customer dissatisfaction. Some clients value a firm's understanding and knowledge of their own company. A square-peg solution will not fit and codified solutions made up of knowledge building bricks are inappropriate here.

Table 10.1 Codification versus personalization strategy (adapted from Hansen *et al.* (1999)).

Feature	Codification	Personalization
Competitive strategy	Produce efficient information systems and robust solutions through the use of codified information, based on past projects.	Produce creative solutions and designs by the incorporation of experts and in-depth needs information from stakeholders.
Economic model	*Reuse economics*: rely on large teams with a high proportion of people highly trained in the reuse of information. Emphasis on the creation of large revenues.	*Expert economics*: make use of small, high-contact teams, carefully chosen and mentored to become partners. Emphasis on maintenance of high profit margins.
Internet strategy	*People-to-documents*: development of an Internet system driven by codified information for project information, company standards and proven design solutions.	*Person-to-person*: create networks that bring together the appropriate stakeholders and subject experts so that tacit knowledge can be exchanged.
Learning strategy	*Create visibility*: emphasis on the transparency of process and product information available as a learning resource. Knowledge is seen as a definable object. Computer-based learning is a viable option.	*Create customer communities*: emphasis on the facilitation of knowledge exchange – knowledge does not exist as a separate entity but as a process. Training through one-to-one mentoring.
Bandwidth	Information in encoded form becomes highly compact and portable for use on the Internet.	Tacit information can only be communicated using high-bandwidth Internet technologies like video conferencing, movies and high-resolution image archives.
Human resources	Reward people for their contribution to the on-line knowledge base.	Reward people for their group contribution of knowledge.
Examples	Bechtel	Haenlein Associates

Some organizations have had their fingers burnt trying to codify their knowledge, only to realize that it does not lend itself to codification – their knowledge is tacit. One example is Xerox who attempted to embed their know-how to support service and repair technicians. The intention was to implement an expert system, installed in copiers that could be used to carry out remote fault diagnoses. However, it soon became apparent that the technicians learned from one another by sharing stories about how they had fixed machines. Their knowledge was tacit.

What next?

Up to this point we have presented a framework for Internet strategy formulation. But perhaps you are asking 'what does it mean for me when I turn up at the design office on Monday?' Or for those taking their first steps in corporate Internet development 'what actions should I take today in preparation for tomorrow?' Perhaps it is worth reminding ourselves of some of the changes aloft that should direct our thinking:

- As the construction value chain fragments and is reconfigured, new business opportunities will arise in the industry.
- The unbundling of the value chain will allow firms to reform in a way that does not compromise their economies of scale and scope.
- Construction services, in order to become accessible to on-line customers, will have to become part of a larger information gateway – a one-stop shop where clients and business-to-business customers can undertake comparative shopping of potential partners, consultants and suppliers. Information gateways or 'portals' may be established by professional bodies (such as the Royal Institute of British Architects who, like other professions, have created on-line directories of members). These navigational sites may be based on databases, but with the advent of intelligent markup languages, search engines will play an increasing role. Information will not be maintained at a single site but will be trawled from all the member sites. For design and construction firms the onus is on them to create on-line information that is intelligible to such search engines. The incorporation of exchange standards and software agents is likely to be a key part of this.
- The Internet will bring about more perfect information in the market. Market operators reliant on the asymmetry of knowledge between clients, subcontractors and manufacturers will find this asymmetry becomes narrowed. Clients and business customers will become more informed and able to bypass firms in the construction value chain, particularly when the 'adding' element disappears!
- The Internet heralds the arrival of open standards in the industry. Previously viewed with suspicion, open software is likely to greatly empower the information technology departments of design and construction firms. Already, the operating system Linux is being rapidly adopted by firms who have come to recognize the perils of proprietary computing systems. With the increasing reliance on company-to-company information exchange, the Internet will be seen as part of a larger migration to open standards right down to the desktop.
- Most of the benefits derived from the Internet will come from design, management and client co-operation. Benefits from on-site use of Internet technology other than for the purposes of reporting are likely to be marginal.

How ready is your business?

Below are some of the key questions that your design or construction firm should be asking when creating an Internet strategy:

- Where on the value chain of our business is information an important component?
- At what point are trade-offs being made between richness and reach?

- Is it possible to extricate certain informational activities to create a stand-alone business?
- Would the separation of the information functions from the business allow the physical business to run more effectively?
- What new services arise in the reshaped value chain?
- What impact does the new 'economics of information' afforded by the Internet have on risk allocation and procurement strategies?
- Can Internet technology coalitions bring about market advantages for partners?
- What current information technology assets are likely to become a liability?
- How is trust to be dealt with from a technological, ethical and competence angle – particularly in an environment of increasingly shared information?
- Does our organization understand the concept of Internet visibility – not just in terms of human access but computer intelligibility as well?

Deep learning

Learning is a term which can easily become a catch-all phrase that means whatever is convenient at the time. However, a new tool with an outdated mind-set is likely to be an ineffective instrument in construction. Learning is a means to an end and its value depends on where it is taking you. Going by the amount of interest shown in bench-marking, learning is increasingly focused on learning about competitors. Hamel and Prahalad (1993) point to some of the dangers of this game of catch-up:

> Too many companies are expending enormous energy simply to reproduce the cost and quality advantages their global competitors already enjoy. Imitation may be the sincerest form of flattery, but it will not lead to competitive revitalization. Strategies based on imitation are transparent to competitors who have already mastered them. Moreover, successful competitors rarely stand still. So it is not surprising that many executives feel trapped in a seemingly endless game of catch-up – regularly surprised by the new accomplishments of their rivals.

As Hawkins (1994) points out, we need to

> move away from the idea that learning just resides within people, and to become aware that learning is also held between people. Relationships, teams, organizations learn and that is not the same as the sum of the learning of all the individuals.

Collective learning systems are complex and dynamic and any Internet system supporting this must reflect this fact. Learning is not a process of knowledge banking – and it is all too often the trap of IT solutions to lead us down this route. Nor is it a set of discrete facts – something which is done separate from and prior to 'doing'. The challenge in Internet development in construction is to develop a variety of understandable maps that distinguish the subtleties which exist between the various levels, cultures, and domains of learning.

People make businesses

With all this talk about technology it is rather tempting to think that the construction industry is replacing people with machines. Nothing could be less true. Today, as always, it is the minds and creativity of the people in the industry that make it such a rewarding industry to be in. Internet technology will provide the tools and access to enable people to harness their skills and reuse existing know-how. An Internet strategy without people at the centre is doomed to fail. Understanding how it facilitates a learning organization is the key to success.

As a final thought is worth looking at the prophesies of Alvin Toffler who, like others, was able to foresee the changes afoot over 30 years ago:

> The day is already in sight when books, magazines, newspapers, films and other media will be offered to the consumer on a design-it-yourself basis. Thus, in the mid-sixties, Joseph Naughton, a mathematician and computer specialist at the University of Pittsburgh, suggested a system that would store a consumer's profile – data about his occupation and interests – in a computer. Machines would then scan newspapers, magazines, video tapes, films and other material, match them against the individual's interest profile, and instantaneously notify him when something appears that concerns him. (Toffler, 1970, *Future Shock*, p. 249)

Little did Toffler know that this form of knowledge management would transform not only the publishing industry but almost every other industry including construction.

So what of construction futurologists? The construction industry needs to attract the very best thinkers to operate in one of the most demanding and complex information environments. Hopefully we will see learning organizations emerging that are capable of nourishing the minds of the most talented individuals.

Directory of expertise – Internet in construction

Introduction

Plenty of leading-edge work is being undertaken by academic and research institutions around the world on the subject of Internet in construction. Much of the work derives from a broad information technology base, but is underpinned by Internet technology. Given the dynamics of the area, this directory points to general schools of research rather than any specific projects. It is arranged by key institutions and identifies particular individuals active in the area. Although the listing is arranged by academic institutions, most of the projects involve some form of industrial participation.

Building Research Establishment, UK (www.bre.co.uk)

Under the direction of Newnham, the Building Research Establishment is investigating the use of intelligent agents in the construction industry for information finding, project support and workflow management. Application domains in which agent solutions are being applied or investigated include workflow management, telecommunications network management, business process reengineering, information retrieval/management, electronic commerce, personal digital assistants, email filtering, digital libraries, command and control, smart databases, and scheduling/diary management.

CSIRO, Australia (www.dbce.csiro.au)

Australia has always been a leading innovator in Internet technology because of the physical expanse of the country itself. At the Centre for Communications in

Construction at CSIRO, John Crawford is heading a project called Global Design Information and Communications in Construction. The project seeks to establish how small and medium sized firms can harness the global potential of networking technology, through the formation of geographically dispersed consortia. The emphasis is on the use of design tools such as electronic whiteboarding, Web-enabled CAD and document markup.

Loughborough University, UK (info.lboro.ac.uk)

The Department of Civil and Building Engineering at Loughborough has a number of Internet-related research projects in its portfolio. Among them are:

- Agent-Based Support for the Collaborative Design of Light Industrial Buildings (ADLIB), led by Anumba and Thorpe;
- Cross-Sectoral Learning in the Virtual Enterprise (CLEVER), led by Anumba and Carillo;
- Integrated Collaborative Design, led by Thorpe, Baldwin and Austin.

The Department is also involved in the Process Protocol research project described in relation to Salford University.

Purdue University, USA (www.tech.purdue.edu/it/resources/aidc)

Duane Dunlap at Purdue University is undertaking interesting work that is particularly relevant to on-site usage of Internet systems. Work includes research in pen-based computing, wireless Internet on-site and 2D bar coding. The website itself provides a useful collection of resources, presentations and links.

Salford University, UK (www.salford.ac.uk)

The Process Protocol project (pp2.dct.salford.ac.uk) is concerned with the development of a common standard in construction projects, relating to IT and process. It is a collaborative project that also involves Loughborough University and industrial partners: Alfred McAlpine (Special Projects) BAA plc., B.T., Advanced Visual Technology Ltd, and Capita. The Process Protocol Map is a comprehensive representation of a construction project from start to finish and is available for download from the website.

Another related project is WISPER (www.aic.salford.ac.uk/Pit). The website provides a test area for integrated construction projects using a Java object-oriented database based on the IFC150final schema (part of the STEP standards).

The Information Technology Institute at the University is also looking at the migration path from document based to model based approaches for information processing in construction projects. Yacine Rezgui and Grahame Cooper describe a system developed around (a) an information management package, (b) a document model package, and (c) a building concept package. Their work is particularly interesting, as it looks at the issues of interworking between dissimilar electronic document management solutions over the Internet. The project involves a consortium of three construction firms, Kvaerner Construction operating in the UK, OTH in France, and JMBygg in Sweden.

Stanford University, Center for Integrated Facility Engineering, USA (www.stanford.edu/group/cife)

The Center for Integrated Facility Engineering (CIFE) is currently pursuing research in the application of advanced technologies aimed at improving the productivity and quality of the architectural, engineering and construction (AEC) industry through increased automation and integration over the lifecycle of a facility. Its second research objective is to pursue research in the management, legal, and business issues associated with the proper selection and implementation of advanced technologies. The Centre is headed by Hans Bjornsson, previously Professor at Chalmers University in Sweden.

Martin Fischer and his team of researchers are developing an area known as four-dimensional (4D) modelling whereby traditional 3D CAD models are combined with construction activities to display the progression of construction over time. The 4D models support computer-based analysis of schedules with respect to cost, interference and safety among others. Researchers in the 4D modelling team are looking at 4D annotation, evaluating buildability, design-cost-schedule integration and time-space conflict analysis.

Also in the CIFE center, in conjunction with UC Berkeley, Renate Fruchter is leading a project called Computer Integrated Architecture, Engineering and Construction. The group is looking at multidisciplinary approaches to AEC design and the creation of a new learning cultures. The course stemming from the project enables Internet-mediated design communication, integration and design frameworks.

A longstanding expert in the area of virtual design teams is Raymond Levitt. The Virtual Design Team (VDT) research was initiated in the late 1980s with the goal of developing new micro-organization theory. This theory is reflected in software tools that are being used at CIFE to design organizations in the same way that engineers design bridges, semiconductors or airplanes.

University of Reading, UK (www.construct.rdg.ac.uk)

The Advanced Construction Technology (ACT) group (www.act.reading.ac.uk), led by Norman Fisher, focuses on the development of knowledge-based generic architectural building and civil engineering models, and on visualization with various advanced CAD and virtual reality systems. In addition it has major projects in the area of benchmarking the cost of ownership and proactive cost modelling.

Also of interest to Internet work is the research on 2D bar coding being undertaken by Roger Flanagan and the author, Edward Finch. 2D bar coding provides a method for low-cost storage of digital data in the form of a label. This gives rise to possibilities of storing Internet files on building products and components. For situations where dial-up access to the Internet is difficult, local web pages provide a user-friendly standard interface. The ability to encode Web links on bar code labels also offers increased integration with manufacturers' on-line help.

University of Hong Kong and Hong Kong Polytechnic University (arch.hku.hk)

Hong Kong has been proactive in the use of Internet technology to foster design skills. Hong Kong University, The Chinese University of Hong Kong and Hong Kong Polytechnic University came together in 1993 to form the Hong Kong Design Teaching and Information Network Group (DING). This network is experimenting with World Wide Web technology for 3D visualization, information management, and the dissemination of design documents including technical standards, product catalogues and slide libraries.

University of Ljubljana, Slovenia (www.fagg.uni-lj.si)

The website for the Faculty of Civil and Geodetic Engineering known as AUDREY (the reason for which remains a mystery) has been an important melting pot for European Internet activities in Europe, starting as early as 1993. The Information Technology in Construction (ITC) server is hosted from this site and provides an experimental research network related to integrated CAD in engineering and architecture. It also provides the home for the innovative on-line *Electronic Journal of Information Technology in Construction*, edited by Ziga Turk – an early proponent of the Internet in construction. The SCENIC database for construction-related research can be accessed from the website and allows searching by organization, projects and publications. Many of the publications are available online.

VTT, Finland (cic.vtt.fi/projects)

VTT is the key research institution related to construction in Finland. Projects it is actively involved with include:

- CONCUR – Concurrent Design and Engineering in Building and Civil Engineering, STEP-based data transfer between inception, design and production.
- ELSWISE – European Large Scale Engineering Wide Integration Support Effort, a method for defining industrial priorities for product data and information technologies.
- RINET – a Web-based building product data library.

Much of the work has been championed by Matti Hannus, a lead researcher in distributed IT applications.

Glossary

Application

Used as a shorter form of 'application program', an application program being a program designed to perform a specific function directly for the user or, in some cases, for another application program. Examples of applications include word processors, database programs, Web browsers, development tools, CAD programs, and communication programs. Applications use the services of the computer's operating system and other supporting applications. The formal requests and means of communicating with other programs that an application program uses is called the application program interface (API).

Application integration

Application integration describes the process of bringing data or a function from one application program together with that of another application program. Object-oriented programming technology makes application integration easier to achieve. With traditional procedural programming, bridge programs had to be written so that one program could work with data or the output from functions in another program. The introduction of object-oriented programming has enabled standard interfaces to be used so that objects designed for use in one application can be reused in other applications.

Application server

An application server is a program on a server in a distributed network that makes elements of an application program available to a wide company audience. Typically tailored to a particular business, it thus provides what is known as the 'business logic'. An application server typically appears in the middle of a three-tier architecture, consisting of a graphical user interface (GUI), the application (business logic) server, and a database and transaction server. An application can thus be divided into three elements:

- a first-tier, Web browser-based graphical user interface, usually at a personal computer or workstation;
- a middle-tier business logic application or set of applications, possibly on a local area network or intranet server;
- a third-tier back-end database and transaction server, sometimes on a mainframe or large server.

Older legacy databases and transaction management applications are part of the back end or third tier. The application server is the middle-man, between browser-based front ends and back-end databases and legacy systems. Often, the application server is used in combination with a Web (HTTP) server and is called a Web application server. The Web browser provides an accessible interface for the user. The Web server provides several different ways to forward a request to an application server and to return a modified or new Web page to the user. Methods include the Common Gateway Interface (CGI), Fast CGI, Microsoft's Active Server Page (ASP), Cold Fusion and the Java Server Page (JSP).

Architecture

In information technology, especially computers and more recently networks, architecture is a term applied to both the process and the outcome of thinking out and specifying the overall structure, logical components, and the logical interrelationships of a computer, its operating system, a network, or other conception. An architecture can be a reference model, such as the Open Systems Interconnection (OSI) reference model, intended as a model for specific product architectures, or it can be a specific product architecture, such as that for an Intel Pentium microprocessor or for IBM's OS/390 operating system.

Computer architecture can be divided into five fundamental components: input/output, storage, communication, control, and processing. In practice, each of these components (sometimes called subsystems) is sometimes said to have an architecture, so, as usual, context contributes to usage and meaning.

By comparison, the term design connotes thinking that has less scope than architecture. An architecture is a design, but most designs are not architectures. A single component or a new function has a design that has to fit within the overall architecture.

A similar term, framework, can be thought of as the structural part of an architecture.

ASP (active server page)

An ASP is an Web (HTML) page that includes one or more scripts (small embedded programs) that are processed on a Microsoft Webserver before the page is sent to the user. An ASP is similar to a server-side include or a common gateway interface (CGI) application in that all involve programs that run on the server, usually tailoring a page in response to specific user requests. Queries from an on-line user result in the retrieval of data from a database which is then built or customized on-the-fly before returning it.

Bandwidth

The bandwidth of a transmitted communications signal is a measure of the range of frequencies the signal occupies. Bandwidth determines the amount of data that can be transmitted or received per unit time. More complex data such as movies consume greater bandwidth. In digital systems, bandwidth can be measured in bits per second (bps). A modem that works at 57 600 bps has twice the bandwidth of a modem that works at 28 800 bps.

Client

A client is both the requesting program or user in a client–server relationship as well as the machine itself that hosts the program. The user of a Web browser is acting as a client when making client requests for pages from servers all over the Web. The computer handling the request and sending back Web pages is a server. Web browsers are the main Internet application used to obtain information on the Internet – and are increasingly used as mail clients as well.

Compiler

A compiler is a program capable of processing statements written in a particular programming language and translating them into machine language that can be processed by a computer. What are known as 'source statements' have to be written in a language such as Pascal or C one line at a time using an editor. The programmer then runs the appropriate language compiler, specifying the name of the file that contains the source statements.

More recently, the Java programming language, an object-oriented language, has introduced the possibility of compiling output (called byte code) that can run on any computer system platform for which a Java virtual machine or byte code interpreter is provided to convert the byte code into instructions that can be executed by the actual hardware processor. This enables Internet users with standard Web browsers to download and run Java applets. These are capable of performing operations just like applications resident on their computer.

EDI (Electronic Data Interchange)

EDI is a standard format for exchanging business data. ANSI X12 is an international standard for EDI and was developed by the Data Interchange Standards Association.

ANSI X12 is closely related to another international standard known as EDIFACT. An EDI message contains a sequential list of data elements, each of which represents a singular piece of information, such as a price, product model or item number. The entire list is called a data segment. One or more data segments contained by a header and trailer form a transaction set, which is the EDI unit of transmission (equivalent to a message). A transaction set often consists of what would usually be contained in a typical business document or form. The parties who exchange EDI transmissions are referred to as trading partners.

Ethernet

Ethernet is the most widely installed local area network (LAN) cabling technology. An Ethernet LAN typically uses coaxial cable or special grades of twisted pair wires. The most commonly installed Ethernet systems are called 10BASE-T and provide transmission speeds up to 10 Mbps. Fast Ethernet or 100BASE-T10 provides transmission speeds of up to 100 Mbsp and is typically used for LAN backbone systems, supporting workstations with 10BASE-T cards. Gigabit Ethernet provides an even higher level of backbone support at 1000 Mbps (1 gigabit or 1 billion bits per second).

Expert system

An expert system is a computer program that reproduces the judgement and behaviour of a human or an organization that has expert knowledge and experience in a particular field. Typically, such a system contains a knowledge base containing accumulated experience and a set of rules for applying the knowledge base to each particular situation that is described to the program. Knowledge elicitation has become an important area of expertise for creating such programs – working in conjunction with the subject expert.

Extranet

An extranet is a private network that uses the Internet protocols to share part of a business's information or operations with suppliers, vendors, partners, customers, or other businesses in a secure way. An extranet can be thought of as being part of a company's intranet that is extended to users outside the company. An extranet requires security and privacy. These requirements are fulfilled by firewall implementation, the use of authentication measures, message encryption, and the use of virtual private networks (VPNs) that tunnel through the public network.

Firewall

A firewall refers to an armoury of programs, located at a network gateway server (a computer that is operating as a gatekeeper between the local network and the Internet proper) that protects the resources of a private network from users outside of the local network. The term also describes the security policy that is used with the programs. An enterprise with an intranet that allows its workers access to the wider Internet presents a potential security risk. Internal computer systems become visible to outside hackers. For this reason it is necessary to install a firewall to prevent outsiders from accessing private data resources and for controlling what outside resources users have access to. A firewall working in conjunction with a router program filters all network packets to determine whether to forward them toward their destination. A firewall typically works with a proxy server that makes network requests on behalf of workstation users. A firewall is often installed in a specially designated computer separate from the rest of the network so that no incoming request can get directly at private network resources.

Gateway

A gateway is a point on a network that acts as an entrance to another network. In a company network, a proxy server acts as a gateway between the internal network and the Internet. A gateway can also be any device that passes packets from one network to another network during passage across the Internet.

Groupware

Groupware refers to programs that enable groups to work together while located remotely from each other. Groupware services may include the sharing of calendars, collaborative authoring tools, email handling, shared database access, electronic meetings and electronic workspace sharing. Product examples of groupware include Lotus Notes and Microsoft Exchange. These programs allow calendar sharing, email handling, and the exchange of files across a networked system so that all users can view the same information. Electronic face-to-face meetings are facilitated by CU-SeeMe and Microsoft NetMeeting.

Hypertext

Hypertext describes the organization of information units into connected associations, shown as highlighted words, that a user can move between. An occurrence of such an association is called a link or hypertext link. Hypertext was one of the main concepts that led to the creation of the World Wide Web. The Web however extends the concept to allow not only local linking but linking to a variety of electronic media dispersed throughout the Internet. The term hypertext was first used by Nelson (1974) in describing his Xanadu system.

Information

Information is a stimulus that has meaning in some context for its receiver. Some kinds of information can be converted into data and passed onto another receiver.

In relation to the computer, we can say that information is (a) made into data, (b) put into the computer where it is stored and processed as data, and (c) put out as data in a form that can be perceived as information.

Inheritance (*see also* OP)

In object-oriented programming, inheritance refers to the concept that when a class of objects is defined, a subclass that is defined acquires the definitions of one or more super-ordinate classes. This means that an object in a subclass does not need to carry its own definition of data and methods that are common to the class (or classes) of which it is a part. This speeds up program development and also helps to ensure validity in structure.

Intelligent agent

On the Internet, an intelligent agent (or simply an agent) is a program that gathers information or performs some autonomous action and on some regular schedule. Typically, an agent program, using parameters provided by an individual, searches all or some part of the Internet, gathers information sought by that individual, and then presents it to that person on a periodic basis. An agent is sometimes called a bot.

Some types of agent act as monitors of specific websites alerting users when the site has been updated or look for specific events (such as a price change). Analyst agents not only gather but also organize and interpret information. The practice or technology of having information brought to an individual by an agent is sometimes referred to as push technology.

Java

Java is a programming language expressly designed for use in the distributed environment of the Internet. It enforces a completely object-oriented view of programming and can be used to create complete applications that run on a single computer or alternatively can be distributed among servers and clients in a network. It can also be used to build small application modules or applets for use as part of a Web page. Applets enable a Web page user to interact with the page.

The Java programs you create are portable in a network. Your program is compiled into Java byte code that can be run anywhere in a network on a server or client that has a Java virtual machine. The Java virtual machine interprets the byte code into code that will run on the real computer hardware. Both of the major Web browsers include a Java virtual machine. Almost all major operating system developers (IBM, Microsoft, and others) have added Java compilers as part of their products. Because Java has no operating system-specific extensions and is an open source language, Java is generally regarded as the most strategic language in which to develop applications for the Web.

List server

A list server (mailing list server) is a program that handles subscription requests for a mailing list and distributes new messages, newsletters, or other postings from the list's members to the entire list of subscribers as they occur or are scheduled. Two commonly used list servers are Listserv and Majordomo.

Newsgroup

A newsgroup is a discussion about a particular subject consisting of notes written to a central Internet site and redistributed through Usenet, a worldwide network of news discussion groups. Usenet uses the Network News Transfer Protocol (NNTP). Newsgroups are arranged according to subject hierarchies, with the first letters of the newsgroup name indicating the major subject category and sub-categories represented by a subtopic name. Users can post to existing newsgroups, respond to previous posts, and create new newsgroups. Newcomers to newsgroups are obliged to familiarize themselves with basic Usenet 'netiquette'. This includes getting familiar with a newsgroup's past discussions before posting to it. An FAQ (frequently asked questions) is provided to avoid repetitious questions. Some newsgroups are moderated by a specific person who decides which postings to allow or to remove, although most newsgroups are unmoderated.

On-the-fly

In relation to computer technology, on-the-fly describes activities that occur dynamically rather than as a result of predefined information stored as flat files on a computer. For example, the content of a page that is sent from a Web site can be embellished on-the-fly using dynamic information such as the time of day, the identity of the user, and specific user input. The Web server calls an application program to produce the on-the-fly page that is to be returned. Techniques for on-the-fly page development include server side includes (SSIs) (often supported by the Web server itself) or systems that allow interaction with desktop applications such as Microsoft's Active Server Page that is typically used to retrieve information from a database.

Ontology

Ontology is the study of what kinds of things exist in the universe. It originates from the Greek *onto* (being) and *logia* (written or spoken discourse). In information technology, an ontology describes the entire set of entities and interactions in some particular domain of knowledge or practices, such as electronic commerce. Tom Gruber, an AI specialist at Stanford University, describes it as 'the specification of conceptualizations, used to help programs and humans share knowledge.' Thought of in this way, an ontology is a set of concepts – such as things, events, and relationships – that are specified in some way (such as specific natural language) in order to create an agreed-upon vocabulary for exchanging information.

OOP (object-oriented programming)

Object-oriented programming relies on objects rather than actions, and uses data rather than logic. In early programming, a program was seen as a logical procedure that takes input data, processes it, and generates output data. The programming preoccupation was how to write the logic, not how to define the data. Object-oriented programming concentrates on objects rather than the logic required to manipulate them. Examples of objects include buildings (described by location, size, structure), assemblies (described by output, power, capacity) or task (described by start time, finish time, duration, resources).

The concept of a data class makes it possible to define subclasses of data objects that share some or all of the main class characteristics. This is known as inheritance, and enables more coherent data analysis, reducing development time, and ensures more accurate coding. As a class defines only the data it needs to be concerned with, when an instance of that class (an object) is run, the code will not be able to accidentally access other program data. This characteristic of data hiding provides greater system security and avoids unintended data corruption. Java is one of the most popular object-oriented languages today and is also the key Internet language.

Open

An open system (as opposed to a proprietary system) is one that conforms to a publicly known and sometimes standard set of interfaces so that anyone using it can also use any other system that adheres to the standard. An open operating system is one for which one can write application programs that will then run on other companies' open operating systems currently or in the future. The best-known open operating system is UNIX, which was allowed to develop as a public venture among some large universities. Operating systems that use the Single UNIX Specification can be considered to be open. The advantages of openness are that users (including programmers and engineers) can learn a single set of skills and find that they are portable across the industry they work in. Likewise, companies will find they can spend less on developing skills for using and working on their own product development. Among a number of organizations that are concerned with promoting open systems is The Open Group. Linux is a modern derivative of UNIX and is an open operating system that is proving to be a very robust platform. It is the favoured operating system for Internet Web servers because of its flexibility and reliability.

Packet

A packet is the discrete item that is routed between a source and a destination on the Internet or any other packet-switched network. When a file (e.g. email message, HTML file, image file) is sent from one place to another on the Internet, the Transmission Control Protocol (TCP) layer of TCP/IP breaks up the file into numerous packets that are an efficient size for routing. Each of these packets is separately numbered and includes the Internet address of the destination. The individual packets for a given file may travel different routes through the Internet. When they have all arrived, they are reassembled into the original file (by the TCP layer at the receiving end). The terms packet and datagram are similar in meaning. A protocol similar to TCP, the User Datagram Protocol (UDP) uses the term datagram.

Parser

A parser is part of a compiler program, and is responsible for receiving sequential inputs from program instructions, interactive on-line commands or markup tags. Using this information it is able to separate the input into categories (for example, the nouns (objects), verbs (methods), and their attributes) that can then be managed by other programs. A parser may also check to see that all the necessary input has been provided. SGML and XML compilers allow the respective documents to be treated in a variety of different ways, so that numerous renditions can be produced from a single information source. An example might be the creation of different renditions for senior managers and middle managers.

Peer-to-peer

Peer-to-peer is a communications model in which each party has the same capabilities and either party can start up a communication session. Other models with which it might be contrasted include the client–server and the master–slave models.

POP (point-of-presence)

A point-of-presence is the location of an access point to the Internet. A POP necessarily has a unique Internet address. A user makes use of a local POP provided by an independent service provider (ISP) or on-line service provider (OSP). Service providers with more POPs are able to provide low-cost connections to more users because of geographical proximity. A POP usually includes routers, digital–analogue call aggregators, servers, frame relay, ISDN (integrated services digital network) or ATM (asynchronous transfer mode) switches.

Scalability

In information technology, scalability has two usages:

- It is the ability of a computer application or product (hardware or software) to continue to function well as it (or its context) is changed in size or volume in order to meet a user need. Typically, the rescaling is to a larger size or volume. The rescaling can be of the product itself (for example, a line of computer systems of different sizes in terms of storage, RAM, and so forth) or in the scalable object's movement to a new context (for example, a new operating system).
- It is the ability not only to function well in the rescaled situation, but to actually take full advantage of it. For example, an application program would be scalable if it could be moved from a smaller to a larger operating system and take full advantage of the larger operating system in terms of performance (user response time and so forth) and the larger number of users that could be handled.

It is usually easier to have scalability upward rather than downward, because developers often must make full use of a system's resources (for example, the amount of disk storage available) when an application is initially coded. Scaling a product downward may mean having to achieve the same results in a more constrained environment.

Server

In general, a server is a computer program that provides services to other computer programs in the same or other computers. The computer in which a server program runs is also frequently referred to as a server (although it may contain a number of server and client programs).

In the server–client model, a server is a program that awaits and fulfils requests from client programs in the same or other computers. A given application in a computer may function as a client with requests for services from other programs and a server of requests from other programs.

Specific to the Web, a Web server is the computer program (housed in a computer) that serves requested HTML pages or files. A Web client is the requesting program associated with the user. The Web browser in your computer is a client that requests HTML files from Web servers.

SGML (standard generalized markup language)

SGML is a standard for how to specify a document markup language or tag set. Such a specification is itself a document type definition (DTD). SGML is not in itself a document language, but a description of how to specify one. It is a meta-language.

SGML is based on the idea that documents have structural and other semantic elements that can be described without reference to how such elements should be displayed. The actual display of such a document may vary, depending on the output medium and style preferences. Some advantages of documents based on SGML are:

- They can be created by thinking in terms of document structure rather than appearance characteristics (which may change over time).
- They will be more portable because an SGML compiler can interpret any document by reference to its document tag definition (DTD).
- Documents originally intended for the print medium can easily be re-adapted for other media, such as the computer display screen.

The language that the Web browser uses, hypertext markup language (HTML), is an example of an SGML-based language. There is a document type definition for HTML (and reading the HTML specification is effectively reading an expanded version of the document type definition).

SGML is based somewhat on earlier generalized markup languages developed at IBM, including general markup language (GML).

TCP (transmission control protocol)

TCP is a method (protocol) used along with the Internet Protocol (IP) to send data in the form of message units between computers over the Internet. Whereas IP takes care of handling the actual delivery of the data, TCP takes care of keeping track of the individual units of data (called packets) that a message is divided into for efficient routing through the Internet.

For example, when an HTML file is sent to you from a Web server, the TCP program layer in that server divides the file into one or more packets, numbers the packets, and then forwards them individually to the IP program layer. Although each packet has the same destination IP address, it may get routed differently through the network. At the other end (the client program in your computer), TCP reassembles the individual packets and waits until they have arrived to forward them to you as a single file.

TCP is known as a connection-oriented protocol, which means that a connection is established and maintained until such time as the message or messages to be exchanged by the application progams at each end have been exchanged. TCP is responsible for ensuring that a message is divided into the packets that IP manages and for reassembling the packets back into the complete message at the other end. In the Open Systems Interconnection (OSI) communication model, TCP is in layer 4, the Transport Layer.

Teleconference

A teleconference is a telephone meeting between two or more participants involving technology more sophisticated than a simple two-way phone connection. At its simplest, a teleconference can be an audio conference with one or both ends of the conference sharing a speaker phone. With considerably more equipment and special arrangements, a teleconference can be a conference, called a videoconference, in which the participants can see still or motion video images of each other. Because of the high bandwidth of video and the opportunity for larger and multiple display screens, a videoconference requires special telecommunication arrangements and a special room at each end. As equipment and high-bandwidth cabling become more commonplace, it is possible that videoconferences will be held from your own computer or even in a mobile setting. One of the special projects of Internet2 is to explore the possibility of having teleconferences in which all participants appear to be in the same room together.

Today's audio teleconferences are sometimes arranged over dial-up phone lines using bridging services that provide the necessary equipment for the call. A special need for some teleconferences is to book and schedule the teleconference room and other resources.

VAN (virtual area network)

VAN is also an acronym for value-added network; also see virtual private network (VPN). A VAN is a network on which users are enabled to share a more visual sense of community through high-bandwidth connections. A VAN is something like a metropolitan area network (MAN) or extended local area network (LAN) in which all users can meet over high-bandwidth connections, enabling 'face-to-face' on-line 'coffee-houses,' remote medical diagnosis and legal consultation, and on-line corporate or extracorporate workgroups, focus groups, and conferences. As the high-bandwidth connections imply a common infrastructure, the first VANs are likely to be local or regional. However, a VAN can also be national or international in geographic scope, assuming all users share similar capabilities.

Virtual organization

A virtual organization or company is one whose members are geographically apart, usually working by computer email and groupware while appearing to others to be a single, unified organization with a real physical location.

VPN (virtual private network)

A VPN is a private data network that makes use of the public telecommunication infrastructure, maintaining privacy through the use of a tunnelling protocol and security procedures. A virtual private network can be contrasted with a system of owned or leased lines that can only be used by one company. The idea of the VPN is to give the company the same capabilities at much lower cost by sharing the public infrastructure. Phone companies have provided secure shared resources for voice messages. A virtual private network makes it possible to have the same secure sharing of public resources for data. Companies today are looking at using a private virtual network for both extranets and wide-area intranets.

Using a VPN involves encrypting data before sending it through the public network and decrypting it at the receiving end. An additional level of security involves encrypting not only the data but also the originating and receiving network addresses. Although as yet there is no standard protocol, Microsoft, 3Com, and several other companies have proposed a standard protocol, the Point-to-Point Tunnelling Protocol (PPTP) and Microsoft has built the protocol into its Windows NT server. VPN software such as Microsoft's PPTP support as well as security software would usually be installed on a company's firewall server.

Virtual reality

Virtual reality is the simulation of a real or imagined environment that can be experienced visually in the three dimensions of width, height, and depth and that may additionally provide an interactive experience visually in full real-time motion with sound and possibly with tactile and other forms of feedback. The simplest form of virtual reality is a 3D image that can be explored interactively at a personal computer, usually by manipulating keys or the mouse so that the content of the image moves in some direction or zooms in or out.

Popular products for creating virtual reality effects on personal computers include Extreme 3D, Ray Dream Studio, 3D Studio MAX, and Visual Reality. The Virtual Reality Modeling Language (VRML) is the *de facto* standard for the Web and allows the creator to specify images and the rules for their display and interaction using textual language statements.

WAN (wide area network)

A WAN is a geographically dispersed telecommunications network: the term distinguishes a broader telecommunication structure from a local area network (LAN). A WAN may be privately owned or rented, but the term usually connotes the inclusion of public (shared user) networks. An intermediate form of network is a metropolitan area network (MAN).

Webcasting (push technology)

Webcasting is the prearranged updating of news, weather, or other selected information on a computer user's desktop interface through periodic and generally unobtrusive transmission over the World Wide Web (including the use of the Web protocol on intranets). Webcasting is a feature of the Microsoft Internet Explorer browser and Netscape's Netcaster, as part of its Communicator suite. Webcasting is also available through separate applications, such as Pointcast and Backweb, that run on current browsers.

Webcasting uses so-called push technology in which the Web server ostensibly pushes information to the user rather than waiting until the user specifically requests it. (In practice, most of the push is triggered by user or administrator preselection and arrives only as the result of client requests.) In addition to changing the Web for the home user, new Webcasting products offer corporations an organized way to manage information for their intranet users.

XML (extensible markup language)

XML is a flexible way to create information formats and share both the format and the data on the World Wide Web, intranets, and elsewhere. For example, computer makers might agree on a standard or common way to describe the information about a computer product (processor speed, memory size, and so forth) and then describe the product information format with XML. Such a standard way of describing data would enable a user to send an intelligent agent (a program) to each computer maker's Web site, gather data, and then make a valid comparison. XML can be used by any individual or group of individuals or companies that want to share information in a consistent way.

XML is currently a formal recommendation from the World Wide Web Consortium as a way to make the Web a more versatile tool. XML is similar to the language of today's Web pages, HTML, in that both contain markup symbols to describe the contents of a page or file. However, HTML describes the content of a Web page (mainly text and graphic images) only in terms of how it is to be displayed and interacted with. For example, a <P> starts a new paragraph. XML describes the content in terms of what data is being described. For example, a <PHONENUM> could indicate that the data that followed it was a phone number. This means that an XML file can be processed purely as data by a program or it can be stored with similar data on another computer or, like an HTML file, that it can be displayed. For example, depending on how the application in the receiving computer wanted to handle the phone number, it could be stored, displayed, or dialled.

XML is *extensible* because, unlike HTML, the markup symbols are unlimited and self-defining. XML is actually a simpler and easier-to-use subset of SGML, the standard for how to create a document structure. It is expected that HTML and XML will be used together in many Web applications.

A more extensive glossary can be obtained online from whatis?com® at www.whatis.com.

References

Akkermans, H., Ygge, F. and Gustavsson. R. (1996) 'HOMEBOTS: Intelligent Decentralized Services for Energy Management', in *Proceedings of The Fourth International Symposium on the Management of Industrial and Corporate Knowledge*, ISMICK '96, Rotterdam, The Netherlands, 21–22 October 1996.

Armour, F.J., Kaisler, S.H. and Liu, S.Y. (1999) 'Building an Enterprise Architecture Step by Step', *IT Professional*, July/August, 31–39.

Baran, P. (1962) *On distributed communications networks*, Rand Corporation.

Bennett, J. and Jayes, S.J. (1995) *Trusting the Team*, Thomas Telford, London.

Bhimani, A. (1996) 'Securing the commercial Internet', *Communications of the ACM*, **39**(6), 29–35.

Chapanis, A., Ochsman, R., Parrish, R. and Weeks, G. (1972) 'Studies in interactive communication: the effects of four communication modes on the behaviour of teams during cooperative problem solving', *Human Factors*, **14**, 487–509.

Coase, R.H. (1937) 'The nature of the firm', *Economica* **4**(4), 386.

Cummings, L.L. and Bromiley, P. (1996) 'The organisational trust inventory (OTI): development and validation', in Kramer, R.M. and Tyler, T.R. (eds), *Trust in Organizations*: *Frontiers of Theory and Research*, Sage, Thousand Oaks, CA, pp. 302–20.

Duyshart, B. (1997) *The digital document*, Butterworth–Heinemann.

Evans, P.B. and Wurster, T.S. (1997) 'Strategy and the new economics of information', *Harvard Business Review*, September–October, 71–82.

Fiol, C. M. and Lyles, M.A. (1985) 'Organisation learning', *Academy of Management Review*, **10**(4), 803–13.

Fish, R., Kraut, R., Root, R. and Rice, R. (1993) 'Video as a technology for informal communication', *Communications of the ACM*, **36**, 48–61.

Gaver, W., Moran, T., MacLean, A., Lovstrand, L., Dourish, P., Carter, K. and Buxton, W. (1992) 'Realising a video environment: EuroParc's RAVE system', in *Proceedings of CHI '92 Human Factors in Computing Systems*, ACM Press, New York, pp. 27–35.

Glushko, R.J., Tenenbaum, J.M. and Meltzer B. (1999) 'An XML Framework for Agent Based E-Commerce', *Communications of the ACM*, **42**(3), 106–114.

Gustavsson, R. (1999) 'Agents with power', *Communications of the ACM*, **42**(3), 41–47.

Guthrie, R. and Austin, L.D. (1996) 'Competitive implications of the Internet', *Information Systems Management*, **13**(3), 90–92.

Hamel, G. and Prahalad, C.K. (1993) 'Strategy as stretch and leverage', *Harvard Business Review*, **71**(2), 75–84.

Handy, C. (1995) 'Trust and the virtual organisation', *Harvard Business Review*, **73**(3), 44–50.

Hansen, M.T., Nohria, N. and Tierney, T. (1999) 'What's your strategy for knowledge management?' *Harvard Business Review*, March–April, 106–116.

Hardwick, M. and Spooner, D.L. (1997) 'Data protocols for the industrial virtual enterprise', *IEEE Internet Computing*, January–February, 20–29.

Hattori, F., Ohguro, T., Yokoo, M., Matsubara, S. and Yoshida, S. (1999) 'Socialware: Multiagent Systems for Supporting Network Communities', *Communications of the ACM*, **42**(3), 55–61.

Hawkins, P. (1994) 'Organisational learning: taking stock and facing the challenge', *Management Learning*, **25**(1), 71–82.

Jain and Singh (1997) 'Using Spheres of Commitment to Support Virtual Enterprises', in *Proceedings of the 4th ISPE International Conference on Concurrent Engineering: Research and Applications (CE)*, Troy, Michigan, August 1997, pp. 469–476.

Jung, C.J. and Hull, R.F.C. (1969) 'On the Nature of the Psyche', in *The Collected Works of Jung Volume 8*, Princeton University Press, NJ, USA.

Kahneman, D. (1973) 'Attention and effort', Prentice-Hall, Englewood Cliffs, NJ.

Kalakota, R. and Whinston, A.B. (1996) *Frontiers of electronic commerce*, Addison-Wesley, Reading, MA.

Kambil, A. (1997) 'Doing business in the wired world', *Computer*, May, 57–61.

Kofman, F. and Senge, P.M. (1993) *Communities of Commitment: The Heart of Learning Organizations*, American Management Association.

Kolb, D.A. (1984) *Experiential learning*, Prentice-Hall, New York.

Kraut, R., Egido, C. and Galegher, J. (1990) 'Patterns of communication in scientific research collaboration', in *Intellectual Teamwork*, (J. Galegher, R. Kraut and C. Egido, eds), Lawrence Erlbaum, Hillsdale, NJ.

Lam, W. (1999) 'Client-Centred Strategies for E-commerce Success', *IT Professional*, September/October, 45–51.

Levitt, B. and March, J.G. (1988) 'Organizational learning', *Annual Review of Sociology*, **14**, 319–340.

Lewicki, R.J. and Bunker, B.B. (1996) 'Developing and maintaining trust in work relationships', in Kramer, R.M. and Tyler, T.R. (eds), *Trust in Organizations: Frontiers of Theory and Research*, Sage, Thousand Oaks, CA, pp. 114–39.

Licklider, J. and Taylor, W. (1968) 'The computer as a Communication Device', *Science and Technology*, April.

Malone, T.W., Yates, J. and Benjamin, I. (1996) 'Electronic markets and electronic hierarchies', *Communications of the ACM*, **30**(6), 484–497.

Mayer, R.C., Davis, J.H. and Schoorman, F.D. (1995) 'An integrative model of organisational trust', *Academy of Management Review*, **20**(3), 709–34.

Mintzberg, H. (1979) *The Structuring of Organizations*, Prentice-Hall, Englewood Cliffs, NJ.

Nelson, T.H. (1974) *Computer Lib/Dream Machines*, Mindful Press, Sausolito, CA.

Nohria, N. and Eccles, R.G. (1992) 'Face-to-face: making network organisations work', in Nohria, N. and Eccles, R.G. (eds), *Networks and Organisations*, Harvard Business School Press, Boston, MA, pp. 288–308.

Panko, R. (1992). 'Managerial communication patterns', *Journal of Organisational Computing*, **2**, 95–122.

Pietroforte, R. (1997) 'Communication and governance in the building process', *Construction Management and Economics*, **15**, 71–82.

Pine, J., Peppers, D. and Rogers, M. (1995) 'Do you want to keep your customers forever?' *Harvard Business Review*, March/April, 103–114.

Porter, M.E. (1996) 'Operational effectiveness is not strategy', *Harvard Business Review*, November/December, 61–78.

Ratnasingham, P. (1998) 'The importance of trust in electronic commerce', *Internet Research*, **8**(4), 313–321.

Rayport, J.F. and Sviokla, J.J. (1995) 'Exploiting the virtual value-chain', *Harvard Business Review*, November–December, 75–85.

Regli, W.C. (1997) 'Internet enabled computer-aided design', *IEEE Internet Computing*, January/February, 39–50.

Reid, A. (1977) 'Comparing the telephone with face-to-face interaction', in (I. Pool, ed.) *The Social Impact of the Telephone*, MIT Press, Cambridge, MA.

Riggins, F.J. and Rhee, H.S. (1998) 'Toward a unified view of electronic commerce', *Communications of the ACM*, **41**(10), 88–95.

Senge, P. (1990) *The Fifth Discipline*, Doubleday.

Shannon, C.E. and Weaver, W. (1999) *The mathematical theory of communication*, University of Illinois Press.

Shapiro, D., Sheppard, B.H. and Cheraskin, L. (1992) 'Business on a handshake', *The Negotiation Journal*, October, 365–78.

Sheldon, T. (1996) *Windows NT Security Handbook*, McGraw-Hill, Osborne.

Short, J., Williams. E. and Christie, (1976) *The Social Psychology of Telecommunications*, John Wiley, London.

Sproull, L. (1984) 'The nature of managerial attention', in L. Sproul and J. Larkey, eds, *Advances in Information Processing in Organisations*, JAI Press, Greenwich, CT.

Strata, R. (1989) 'Organisational learning – the key to management innovation', *Sloan Management Review*, Spring, 63–4.

Tang, J. and Rua, M. (1994) 'Montage: providing teleproximity for distributed groups', in *Proceedings of CHI '94 Human Factors in Computing Systems*, pp. 37–43, ACM Press, New York, NY.

Toffler, A. (1970) *Future Shock*, The Bodley Head, London.

Walther, J.B. (1995) 'Relational aspects of computer-mediated communication: experimental observations over time', *Organization Science*, **6**(2), 186–203.

Williamson, O.E. (1975) *Markets and hierarchies: Analysis and antitrust implications*, Free Press, New York.

Whittaker, S. and O'Conaill, B. (1993) 'Evaluating videoconferencing', in *Companion Proceedings of CHI '93 Human Factors in Computer Systems*, ACM Press, New York, NY.

Whittaker, S. (1995) 'Rethinking video as a technology for interpersonal communications: theory and design implications', *Int. J. Human Computer Studies*, **42**, 501–529.

Wigand, R.T. (1997) 'Electronic commerce: definition, theory and context', *The Information Society*, **13**(3), 1–16.

Zwass, V. (1996) 'Electronic commerce: structures and issues', *Intern. J. Electr. Comm.* **1**(1), 3–23.

Index

Active Server Pages 30
activity-system map 25
AECinform 74
aecXML 120
agents 56, 79, 106
AllView 114
application programming interfaces (APIs) 119
architects 69
Astoria 135
asymmetric keys 88
auctioning 108

bandwidth 20
baseline definition 140
baseline views 143
Bechtel 31
BecWeb 33
briefing 71
brokering 108
buying agent 107
buying process 101

CAD 6, 42
CERN 37
CITE 103
codification 6, 151
cognitive cueing 61
collections 129
community 9, 69
CommunityOrganizer 80
COMPASS 72
competitive convergence 23
components 129
conference boards 74
content management 131
CORBA 52
cryptography 88
customization 20

data protocols 52
data 3
deep learning 8, 155
Design Build 75
document management 65
DTD 36, 124
dynamic model 30

eavesdropping 86
eCo System 104
e-commerce framework 112
e-commerce 100
economics of information 19
EDI 100
EDICON 103
educational building 71
encryption 32, 88
enterprise architecture 139
estimating 33
experiential learning 29
expert systems 35
expertise 157
extranets 113

façade systems 5
face-to-face interaction 57
firewalls 90, 93

gas-fired power stations 65
Generic Design and Construction Process
    Protocol 16

Hans Haenlein Architects 69
holism 8
hyperarchy 22

industrial virtual enterprise 53
information transfer 2

inheritance 49
interactivity 20
InterCAP 47
interoperability 57
interorganizational systems (IOS) 111
intronets 113

Java 52

lean information 6
learning organization 2, 7
legacy systems 33
list servers 73
load balancing 109

marketplace 16
marketspace 16
mobile agents 106
monitoring agent 107

namespace 124
negotiation 108
neutral file formats 118
newsgroups 74
non-verbal communication 60, 63

object linking and embedding (OLE) 51
object modelling 49
on-line discussion 74
open standards 19
operational effectiveness (OE) 23
organization learning *see* learning organization

parameterization 50
parsing 39
partnering 94
password sniffing 86
physical value chain (PVC) 18
private key 88
process coordination 59
procurement 33
product data management (PDM) 44
productivity frontier 24
project databases 119
project development 141
protocol 54
proxy server gateways 92
public key 88

real-time video 60

repudiation 87
RIBA directory 72
rich information 6
roll-out 34

schema 123
scoping 141
screening routers 91
SGML 36
smart home 109
SMART project 110
social cueing 62
socialware 79
software agents *see* agents
sphere of commitment 110
spoofing 87
stateful inspection 93
statement of need 69
static model 30
STEP 46, 53, 126
strategic fit 25
strategic positioning 24
supronets 113

tacit knowledge 151
target definition 140
target vision 142
Taywood Engineering 64
telemetry 67
thin-client 30
thinking 11
transaction costs 22, 84
trust model 96
trust 83
turn-taking 62

video as data 60
video for connection 60, 63
virtual private networks 32, 94
virtual value chain (VVC) 18
virtuality 84

Whip 46
wide area network 32

XML databases 131
XML fragment 39
XML 37, 104, 124

zero-sum 23